REMEMBER LOT'S WIFE

And Other Unnamed
Women of the Bible

by April Yamasaki

faithQuest
Elgin, IL

Published by *faithQuest*, an imprint of Brethren Press, 1451 Dundee Avenue, Elgin, IL 60120

Cover design by Jeane Healy

Cover illustration reprinted from *God's Images* by James Dickey and Marvin Hayes, Oxmoor House. Reprinted with permission of the publisher.

98   97   96   95   94   5   4   3   2

Library of Congress Cataloguing-in-Publication Data

Yamasaki, April.
    Remember Lot's wife: and other unnamed women of the Bible/April
    Yamasaki.
        p.cm.
    ISBN 0-87178-734-2
    1. Women in the Bible—Meditations. 2. Devotional calendars. I. title
BS575.Y36   1991
220.9'2—dc20   90-48224

Manufactured in the United States of America

Do not fear, for I have redeemed you; I have called you by my name, you are mine. When you pass through the waters, I will be with you; and through the rivers, they shall not overwhelm you; when you walk through fire you shall not be burned, and the flame shall not consume you. For I am the Lord your God, the Holy One of Israel, your Savior.

Isaiah 43:1b-3a

Contents

Introduction

From the opening chapter of Genesis to the closing words of Revelation, the Bible bears witness to the importance of names. In the beginning, God created light and darkness, heaven and water and dry land, and God named them Day and Night, Sky and Seas and Earth. In the last chapter of Revelation, Jesus gives his own names as the Alpha and Omega, the first and the last, the beginning and the end, the root and descendant of David, the bright morning star.

Throughout the Bible, the names of people and places receive careful attention. The book of Numbers lists all the people of Israel by family name. Paul's letter to the Romans ends with greetings to various Christians by name. In both the Old and New Testaments, people often receive names that express their personality or the events surrounding their birth. The names of places are carefully explained.

Given this wealth of names recorded in the Bible, it is all the more striking to discover how many names are missing from its pages, particularly the names of women. In the biblical genealogies, for example, women's names were regularly omitted as part of the tradition of patriarchy. In other places, women are mentioned but unnamed. Like Lot's wife, some of these unnamed women of the Bible played a relatively small part in a much larger story. Like the poor widow at the temple treasury, some women were never identified to the biblical writers. Like Samson's mother, some women stood in the shadow of more well-known family members.

Unfortunately, and with few exceptions, these unnamed women of the Bible have too often become unmentioned and unremembered women. We may have heard a sermon or two on the Samaritan woman at the well, but who remembers the bent woman healed on the Sabbath or Philip's four prophesying daughters? What about the wise woman of Tekoa and the widow of Zarephath? Their stories may be unfamiliar to us, yet from the biblical record it is clear that they and many other unnamed women made a difference in the lives of people around them and in the history of their world. They have their own stories to tell and their own lessons to teach us.

Like many of these biblical women, many of us will be unnamed in the history books written about our own age. And many of us may feel unnamed in the life situations we face. We are the youngest Smith daughter or John's wife or Gloria's mother or the office secretary or the grade-five teacher or the family doctor or the woman in red who wants a refund at the department store counter.

Sometimes we may honestly find it easier to remain anonymous. We may not feel the need to identify ourselves completely to everyone we meet. We are content to be John's wife when his office calls or to be Gloria's mother when we visit our child's school. We are thankful for our various relationships with other people and for the various roles we play in their lives.

But sometimes it can be wearing, even demeaning, to be identified always by our relationship to someone or something else. Sometimes being unnamed can make us feel unloved, unwanted, unworthy. We feel ourselves shrinking in significance to God and to other people.

Yet nothing could be further from the truth. As God called our biblical foremothers to a life of faith, so God also calls us. As God loved them and knew their names, so God also loves and names us. We too make a difference in the world around us. We too have our own stories to tell.

On the following pages, I invite you to meet some of the unnamed women of the Bible and to connect their stories with your own. Each woman is brought into focus with a Scripture reference, a reflection on the Scripture, a meditation focus, and a short prayer. The reflections are not sermons or full biographies. Instead, they are introductions, starting points, kindling for the fire of your own thoughts about God, yourself, and other people. For further reflection and study, some suggestions for journaling and group activities appear at the end of the book along with a list of resources.

May these pages enrich your own journey of faith and bring you a deeper appreciation for these women of the Bible. God knows their names. God knows our names too.

April Yamasaki

Letting Go

Scripture Reading: Genesis 19:15-26

I know why Lot's wife looked back. It was not so much curiosity, the way some people today follow fire trucks or slow their cars at the scene of an accident on the street. It was not so much a longing for some secret pleasure or earthly wealth, as one might expect given the reputation of Sodom. No, it was something much closer to ordinary life and much closer to our own experience.

We must back up a bit first and note how very little the Bible tells us about Lot's wife—only that she looked back on the destruction of Sodom and became a pillar of salt. But since the Bible only mentions her after Lot had settled in Sodom, we might well think of Lot's wife as a native of that town.

Imagine Sodom as her home. The people were her family, friends, and neighbors. She was born there and had her two daughters there. She had lived in the same house for years, ever since she had married Lot. She drew water from the same well every day. She knew the streets of the town as she knew her own backyard. And that is why Lot's wife looked back.

One day her life was filled with the ordinary activities of eating, drinking, planting, and making a home, and the next day two strangers told her she had to leave all of that behind. She had no time to pack. No time to say goodbye. The strangers said she should not even look back on the town for one last time.

Lot's wife spent a sleepless night. She repeated the strangers' words over and over in her mind. In the morning she did leave without packing. She did leave without a final visit to the well or a tearful goodbye to her friends and neighbors. But she could not quite bring herself to leave without a backward glance.

She was too attached to her past, too rooted there. She could not leave it behind. And so instead, Lot's wife looked back, and in that instant paid a heavy price, for she also gave up the new future that God had planned for her. She became a pillar of salt, frozen in time between the past and the future, between what used to be and what might have been.

Like Lot's wife, we all look back. Sometimes that can be fun and even necessary. We enjoy old photographs, vacation souvenirs, and school reunions. We draw strength from past accomplishments and learn from past mistakes. Our past can be a healthy foundation for our present and for our future. Our past can help us to grow and change and to be the people that God calls us to be.

But while there is a time for savoring memories and for building on the past, there is also a time for letting go. Like Lot's wife, sometimes we too must leave the past behind and go forward in response to God's call. When we marry, we need to leave the single life behind. When we move to a new city, we need to get acquainted with a new neighborhood and to make new friends, instead of forever longing for our old ones. When we work together in the church, sometimes we need to discard the old wineskins and adapt new ways of doing things.

At such times, we may be tempted to a kind of looking back that comes too close to the example of Lot's wife. We may be too attached to our past in ways that are unhealthy, that paralyze us, and prevent us from moving forward. We hold on to the past and refuse to change. We fill our lives with regret for what used to be. We concentrate so much on looking back over our shoulders, that we stumble, fall, and lose sight of the new future that God has planned for us.

And so in our own lives, we need to remember Lot's wife. When God calls us, let us answer. If we try to save our life, we will lose it. If we cling too tightly to the past, we will have no future. Let us move ahead. God is calling.

Meditation Focus: What are some healthy ways of remembering and appreciating your past? What are some unhealthy ways of looking back?

Prayer: O God, free us to follow your call in our lives. Help us to let go of the past where it threatens to paralyze our growth as your people. Teach us to remember and to appreciate the past where it enriches our present and enables us to face the future. Amen.

Strong Women

Scripture Reading: Genesis 19:30–38

Many of us would gladly ignore the story of Lot's daughters. We would rather not talk about such a tale of sex and exploitation, of drunkenness and incest. Its subject matter makes us uncomfortable. Its directness embarrasses us. Such an appalling account would seem more at home on the pages of a modern city tabloid than in the holy Scriptures.

At the very least, we expect the Bible to provide some sort of moral to the story, some word of judgment. But no moral appears, and no judgment is passed. Other passages of Scripture talk about healthy sexual expression, rebuke exploitation, and condemn drunkenness and incest; but here the Bible provides no comment on all these issues.

Why then is this story preserved in the pages of the Bible? Is it simply to explain the origins of the Moabites and the Ammonites? Is it to show us Lot's ultimate falling away from God's will? The story of Lot's daughters presents many more questions than it answers.

The Bible simply records the story of two women and how they handled their very unusual situation. At the time of Sodom's destruction, they had fled the city with their mother and father. Their mother made the mistake of looking back on the city; their father hurried them to Zoar, where they lived only briefly before moving into the mountains. Alone in this isolated place with their father, the two women realized that they could not marry and bear children. And so at the suggestion of the older daughter, the two decided on a plan to have children by their father.

Perhaps the two women were lonely. Or perhaps they simply longed for children and for some semblance of ordinary human life. They may have feared for the preservation of their family line or even for the continuation of the whole human race. Whatever their motivation, the two women took stock of their situation, devised a plan of action, and successfully carried it out.

Earlier in the Genesis narrative, the two daughters had remained very much in the background, only mentioned by Lot when he tried to calm the crowd at his door. In this part of Lot's story, however, they take the foreground and become fully developed characters with wills and plans of their own. Earlier in the narrative, Lot had been the main actor; here he was the passive one, unaware of his daughters' plans, in a drunken stupor when they took advantage of him, and unmentioned at the birth and naming of his grandsons. Once Lot would have used his daughters to satisfy an angry mob; now they used his body to satisfy their own desires.

We might admire the two women for their resourcefulness, for their ability to make the best of an impossible situation. They were independent and intelligent, creative and clever. Instead of fear, they had hope. Instead of being depressed or passive, they took decisive action. But in spite of all of these positive sides to their characters and to their story, it is clear that something—someone—is missing. In the whole narrative, God is not mentioned at all.

When the older daughter spoke, she spoke only with her younger sister. When the two women acted, they acted on their own. God did not speak to them or take part in their decision. And perhaps God's very absence from the story implies a certain moral: Human strength and human decision-making need to be exercised in the context of God's will and with respect for others.

From history and from our own experience, we know that women are resourceful, independent, strong, able to assess situations and to respond to them. We know that we ourselves are intelligent and creative. We have a wonderful ability to identify problems, to think them through, to arrive at solutions, and to carry them out.

But as God's people, we cannot rely on these strengths alone or use them only for our own desires; we cannot follow the example of Lot's daughters. Instead, let us seek God's direction for our lives and follow "what is good and acceptable and perfect" (Rom. 12:2b).

Meditation Focus:What strengths has God given you? How can you use them for God? How can you exercise them with respect for others?

Prayer: O God, we thank you for the many strong women you have given us in our families and throughout history. Thank you for the strengths you have given us, for the gifts of thinking and planning and acting. May we use them wisely according to your will and with respect for others. Amen.

In the Company of Women

Scripture Reading: Exodus 2:1–10

The story of the Exodus is the story of women. In chapter one, two Hebrew midwives begin the drama with their refusal to obey the Pharaoh's order to kill all the newborn Hebrew boys. Now here in chapter two, several more women act to save the infant Moses: Moses' mother, Moses' sister, Pharaoh's daughter, and her attendants. Without these women, there would have been no Moses and perhaps no Exodus at all.

Apart from their concern for Moses, these unnamed women had little in common. Two were Hebrews, the rest Egyptians. One was a member of the royal family; the others were common folk or servants. One was a mother; one was only a child.

In this reflection we focus on just one of these unique, but unnamed, actors: the young Hebrew girl, who was Moses' sister. While the girl remains unnamed in this passage of Scripture, the biblical genealogies call Moses' only sister Miriam (Num. 26:59; 1 Chron. 6:3). And from later accounts, we see that Miriam would grow up to become a leader of the Hebrews during their Exodus from Egypt (Exod. 15:20-21; Mic. 6:4).

But at the time of our Scripture reading, the young Miriam and the rest of her family still lived in captivity. Once the Hebrew people had been welcomed and accepted in Egypt as descendants of Joseph. But now they suffered under hard labor imposed on them by the Egyptians. In fact, they were so feared and hated that the Pharaoh passed a death sentence on all infant boys born to the Hebrews; only the female children were allowed to live.

Ironically, it was a girl child—Moses' unnamed sister—who played a leading role in spoiling Pharaoh's plans. After Moses' mother placed Moses in the river, it was Miriam who watched over his basket to see what would happen. When Pharaoh's daughter opened the basket and discovered the crying boy, it was Miriam who suggested that she hire a Hebrew nurse to care for him. Even as a young, unnamed girl, Miriam showed the initiative that would one day make her a leader of the Hebrew people.

While Miriam's story is an ancient one, it is also unfortunately very contemporary. The extreme circumstances of oppression which she faced are with us still in various parts of the world. Like the ancient Hebrews, some peoples today still suffer the systematic attempts of others to destroy their culture, their livelihood, their children, their physical life. Nations still oppress nations, and governments still rule unjustly.

For those who suffer under such oppression, the story of Miriam stands as an example of positive action in oppressive circumstances. Although she was young, she did what she could. Although she was only one individual, she exercised what power of courage and creativity that she possessed. She could not immediately change the circumstances of her people's oppression, but she would not stand idly by. Instead, she did what she could and prepared the way for freedom.

For those of us who have been spared such oppression, the story of the young Miriam stands as an invitation to join with all oppressed peoples. Like Moses' sister, we can watch over the events of our world to see what will happen. Like her, we can remain informed and ready to act. We can offer creative solutions to those in authority. We can use our economic and political power to take positive action.

Above all, we can remember that we do not act alone. For all her initiative, Miriam did not act alone in saving Moses. Her mother made the reed basket, committed him to the waters, and later became his nurse. The Pharaoh's daughter took the child from the river, paid his mother to nurse him, and brought him into the royal household. Miriam was part of a whole company of women whose independent efforts combined to save Moses. In the same way, we do not work alone, but with and for many others.

Meditation Focus: What situations of oppression are you aware of in our world? How can you keep yourself informed and available for action?

Prayer: O God of the poor and oppressed, when we see the suffering of our world, we are tempted to feel discouraged and powerless. But may we take heart from the story of Miriam. As she took positive action in her circumstances, may we also have the boldness and creativity to work for peace and justice today. And may we remember that, like her, we do not act alone. Amen.

Egypt Revisited

Scripture Reading: Exodus 2:1–10

Yes, once again we return to Egypt. And no, the Scripture reading that heads this reflection is no misprint. Moses' birth is so important, and the involvement of unnamed women in his story so crucial, that this portion of Scripture is worth re-reading and re-thinking once more. This time, however, we focus not on Moses' sister, but on the unnamed woman who would become Moses' second mother.

Moses' adopted mother was a daughter of the Egyptian Pharaoh. Although she makes only this one brief appearance in the biblical narrative, her role was an important one in shaping biblical history. Like Moses' sister, Pharaoh's daughter also helped to prepare the way for Hebrew freedom. She too defied Egyptian law and so helped to save the life of the Hebrew infant who would one day lead his people out of Egypt.

We might have expected a member of Moses' own family to act on his behalf. And we might even have expected the Hebrew women as a group to protect their Hebrew children. After all, the family was a basic unit of the Hebrew people, and it was only natural for the people to try to preserve it. So as we might have expected, the two Hebrew midwives named Shiphrah and Puah (1:15–21), Moses' mother, and Moses' sister all defied the Pharaoh's edict.

But what is surprising is the involvement of the Pharaoh's own daughter and her servants. According to the biblical text, Pharaoh's order to kill all of the male infants born to the Hebrews had clearly gone out to all the people (1:22). Everyone— including Pharaoh's daughter and her servants—must have been well aware of the Pharaoh's word. But in spite of that knowledge, these unnamed Egyptian women decided to save the Hebrew boy.

Pharaoh's daughter did not simply take the child from the water, but also made him her own adopted son. And when the boy was old enough, she included him in her household. She not only accepted the child's right to live, but accepted him as part of her own family.

In her decision to raise Moses as her own, Pharaoh's daughter took a significant risk. In the ancient world, it was bad enough for a daughter to defy her father's wishes; it was even worse for the daughter of a Pharaoh. Her disobedience was not simply a matter within the family, but a matter of national law and order.

Why did Pharaoh's daughter choose to save Moses and to disobey her father? Why did she go to such trouble to provide Moses with a hired nurse and to give him a place in her household?

Our text suggests that Pharaoh's daughter was moved by compassion for the child, for it tells us that Pharaoh's daughter opened the basket, saw Moses crying, and took pity on him (v. 6). Her compassion was not simply a warm feeling of sympathy. It was an active, risk-taking, long-term commitment. It was a compassion unrestricted by law, by ethnic difference, or by social status. It was a compassion that moved her to risk her father's anger and to break her father's law.

Today we too have plenty of opportunity to show compassion to others. In our own world, there are still people who suffer under oppressive governments. There are still babies whose lives are threatened by exposure, violence, poverty, and hunger. Sometimes our compassion may lead us into service vocations, like medicine or social work, teaching or pastoring. Sometimes our compassion may lead us into political action and civil disobedience, like the organization of a women's shelter or the non-payment of war taxes.

Like Pharaoh's daughter, we too can be compassionate people. We can be active rather than passive, risk-takers rather than bystanders, people of long-term commitment rather than people with passing fancy. We too can help make a difference in our world.

Meditation Focus: How could you express compassion for someone else today? How could you express compassion in a long-term commitment?

Prayer: We can be people of compassion, for God first had compassion on us. God took action to create us as unique individuals, took the risk of becoming human for our sake, and continues to be committed to our well-being. May we in turn show compassion for others with the strength, courage, and endurance granted by God. Amen.

Building for Eternity

Scripture Reading: Exodus 35:20–29

Throughout the biblical story, both men and women share equally in spiritual life and responsibility. Genesis tells us that both men and women were created in the image of God. The gospels report the experiences of both men and women who travelled with Jesus. In the book of Acts and the letters of the early church, we see how both served as leaders of the early Christian communities.

Here also in the building of the tabernacle, both men and women participated freely. They both gathered together before Moses and received the instructions which he had received from God on the mountaintop. They both felt God speak in their own hearts and stir their own spirits.

Like the men of the Exodus, the women responded to God's call with an offering of articles that could be used to build the tabernacle. They brought out the fine linens and colorful yarns that they had carried with them from Egypt. They offered the earrings and neck ornaments that they had received from their Egyptian neighbors. They even brought their household and personal articles that could be used for their silver and brass.

In addition, the women gave their time and artistic skills. They brought their knowledge and experience as weavers, their love for color and texture. As they gave what they could, they also did what they could. Under their capable and willing hands, the tabernacle and its furnishings took shape.

This giving of the Exodus women was a total one, embracing both what they owned and what they could do, their possessions and themselves. Without their involvement, the tabernacle would have had no curtains and no gold clasps to join the curtains together. The tabernacle would have remained just a heavenly vision instead of a real place of worship.

As the women worked on the tabernacle and its furnishings, they worked at an important—but ultimately earthly—task. The tabernacle would become the focal point of Israel's worship and the main symbol of God's presence in the community. But it would also remain an earthly structure, subject to capture and loss.

And so the women's enduring work was not the tabernacle; no, their enduring work was the community they built around it. They heard God's word and obeyed. They responded to God's Spirit and gave their best to the work of the tabernacle. By their faithfulness, they built up the community of faith. They set an example for one another as people of worship who were responsive to God's word and leading.

Like the women of the Exodus, we too participate in the building and furnishing of our own places of worship. We give our money to build church buildings. We spend our time making floral arrangements and special holiday displays. We use our talents to make banners for our sanctuaries and cloths for our communion tables. As we participate in the life of the church in these ways, we stand in the noble tradition of the women of the Exodus who built the tabernacle.

Like their work, this work of ours is also important when we do it in response to God's leading and with the purpose of enriching our worship. But this work is also earthly and temporary. Church buildings do not last forever. The floral arrangements and special displays need to be replaced. The banners and table cloths wear out with repeated use and launderings.

Our more important work is the one that lies behind these physical things. Like the women of the Exodus, our lasting work is not a place of worship, but a people of worship. We too are building a community of people who will hear and obey God's word, who will be responsive to God's Spirit, who will be people of worship. We are building this more lasting tabernacle, this more lasting church, which is the community of faith. We are building for eternity.

Meditation Focus: How is God's Spirit stirring your heart to work within the community of faith? How will you build for eternity?

Prayer: Spirit of God, who moved among the women of the Exodus, move also among us. Help us to value that tradition of service and community building started so long ago and continued throughout history by countless unnamed women. May we follow their example of faith and obedience as we work within the community of faith today. In the name of Jesus, who stands at the center of our life and worship. Amen.

Blessed are Those Who Mourn

Scripture Reading: Judges 11:34-40

Of all the stories in the Bible, the tale of Jephthah's daughter is one of the most tragic. What should have been a joyous homecoming became a time of great sorrow. The news of Jephthah's vow soon turned his daughter's dancing into mourning, her robes of gladness into sackcloth.

This story of father and daughter is so painful, so unbelievable, that many have tried to find a less terrible ending. Perhaps Jephthah's vow did not really mean death for his daughter. Perhaps the sacrifice meant only that she remained unmarried for the rest of her life.

But while such explanations might sound somewhat more acceptable to us, nothing in the text itself suggests that Jephthah did any less than sacrifice his daughter.

Even though human sacrifice went against the law of Moses (Deut. 12:31), it was certainly practiced at times among the pagan nations and even in Israel (e.g., 2 Kings 16:3; 17:17). And the time of Jephthah and the rest of the judges of Israel was itself a lawless time: "all the people did what was right in their own eyes" (21:25).

In the eyes of both Jephthah and his daughter, the right thing was for Jephthah to keep his cruel vow. Jephthah's daughter would not marry, have children and grandchildren. She would not enjoy the victory of her people and the years of peace that would come to them under the leadership of her father. Her life would end before her adult life had even begun.

In his despair, Jephthah cried out to his daughter, "You have brought me very low" (v. 35). He acted as if she were to blame, as if he himself had not been the author of their troubles, as if the sacrifice were his alone.

But Jephthah's daughter did not retaliate by blaming him in return. There is no trace of tears or panic or complaint on her part. In spite of the very personal and terrifying consequences, she affirmed her father's need to keep his vow. She answered his despairing words with her own calm and courageous words accepting her fate.

At the same time, however, Jephthah's daughter did not accept the role of passive victim. Although she would not and could not change her father's vow, she did not suffer in silence or meekly surrender. Instead, she responded with words of her own, with a request to go to the mountains, to spend time in the company of friends, to mourn the loss of her life.

Today we would call Jephthah's vow cruel, and its fulfillment the height of child abuse. We do not accept such authority of father over daughter. We reject the literal and physical sacrifice of human life even in the name of religion.

But if we consider the broad outlines of this story, we find that it is not quite as foreign to our own experience as it first appears. Like Jephthah's daughter, sometimes we too experience circumstances beyond our control. We too face situations in which life as we know it must come to an end.

The loss of a family member or friend through death changes the shape of our home and personal lives. An unexpected pregnancy or an unexpected inability to conceive changes our idea of family. Illness or accident may cut short the dreams and expectations we hold for our own lives.

Like Jephthah, our first response might be one of despair and blaming other people for our situation. We might panic or complain. Or we might go to the other extreme and meekly go along with events, suffering in silence, burying our grief in busyness, pretending that everything is fine even while our lives are falling apart.

But at those points of crisis, we need to remember the example of Jephthah's daughter. We are not passive victims. We are not without spiritual resources. We need to take time to be with God on our own mountain of prayer, to seek out supportive friends, to reflect on and mourn the passing of time and the changes in our lives. As Jesus reminds us, "Blessed are those who mourn, for they will be comforted" (Matt. 5:4).

Meditation Focus: What circumstances beyond your control have you experienced in your own life? In what ways have you allowed yourself to mourn?

Prayer: God of all comfort, be with us through the changing circumstances of our lives. Help us to face them with courage and with the sure knowledge of your presence. Amen.

Honored by God

Scripture Reading: Judges 13:2-24

For a woman in biblical times, the only thing worse than not having sons was not bearing children at all. Without children, a woman was cut off from her own hopes and dreams for marriage and family life and from feeling good about herself and her body. She might be divorced by her husband or forced to share him with a second wife or concubine. She might be criticized by her extended family and looked down upon by other women. Without children, she might even doubt her relationship with God, for children were regarded as a sign of God's blessing, and the absence of children a sign of God's displeasure. In fact, to be childless was so painful, that the childless Rachel could turn to her husband and say, "Give me children, or I shall die" (Gen. 30:1).

As a childless woman, Manoah's wife might well have identified with Rachel's desperate plea. She too was something of an outcast in her own society, her own religion, her own home. She too must have struggled with deep personal, interpersonal, and spiritual questions.

But to God, Manoah's wife was no outcast. In fact, her encounter with God's messenger suggests that God took special care to treat her with respect.

To begin with, let us note that God's messenger appeared first to Manoah's wife and not to her husband. In a patriarchal culture which honored men over women, we might have expected just the opposite. Furthermore, in a culture which tended to equate barrenness with sinfulness, the angel's appearance to Manoah's wife was even more striking. By sending the messenger to Manoah's wife, God honored her and affirmed her worth.

Later, when Manoah prayed for God to send the messenger again, God answered his prayer indirectly by again sending the messenger to his wife. God did not bypass Manoah's wife in favor of her husband. Instead, God favored her with the messenger's second appearance.

Finally, when Manoah himself spoke to God's messenger, the angel merely repeated the earlier message and added nothing new. Even the words "all that I said to her" (v. 13) and "everything that I commanded her" (v. 14) emphasized the woman's first encounter with the angel. It was almost as if God gave Manoah an unspoken rebuke for not simply believing his wife the first time.

So throughout the story, God treated Manoah's wife as a person worthy to receive the word of the Lord, and Manoah's wife proved worthy of that honor. While her husband seemed frightened and confused at times, she calmly affirmed what she had seen and heard and went about preparing for the child she knew that she would bear.

Today childlessness is not what it was in the days of Manoah's wife. It is no longer grounds for divorce. It is not as often interpreted as a sign of God's displeasure. For some women, it is even regarded as a matter of choice. Yet even today, unwanted childlessness is often personally devastating, a terrible blow to one's dreams, a source of tension in one's marriage and extended family. For some of us, unwanted childlessness may be a time of intense personal, interrelational, and spiritual crisis.

For others, crisis comes through the experience of being single, or the loss of a job, or a move to a new city, the death of a family member, the betrayal of a friend, a miscarriage, depression. All of us have experiences that cause us to question our own worth, that make us feel cut off from our friends and family, that make us uncertain about our relationship with God.

These are times when we might long for a messenger from heaven to speak God's word to us; when life seems so hard that, like Rachel, we cry out for relief or death; when we feel we simply cannot go on.

And that is exactly where God meets us. We may not always get the child or the new job or whatever it is that we think we need. Our ways are not God's ways. But as God loved and honored the wife of Manoah, so God loves and honors us. God speaks to us through the Scriptures, through other people, through our prayers. God stands with us through every crisis.

Meditation Focus: What points of crisis can you identify in your own life? How did God meet your needs?

Prayer: O God, we thank you for your loving presence throughout all life's difficulties. Like Manoah's wife, may we be quick to hear your word and to act on your promises. In the name of Jesus, who is God with us. Amen.

Speaking Out

Scripture Reading: Judges 19:1-30

It hardly seems fair to call the woman of this story the Levite's concubine, for the Levite treated her with unspeakable cruelty. In Bethlehem, he spent more time with her father than he did with her. In Gibeah, he forced her out of the house to be raped and beaten by the men of the city. In Ephraim, he cut her dead body in pieces, denied her a decent burial, and sent her limbs throughout Israel. From first to last, the Levite expressed no concern for her welfare; he cared more for his donkeys than he did for his woman.

So let this woman—this unnamed, unloved, mistreated, abused, gang-raped, murdered, mutilated woman—let this woman not be known only in relation to her master. Let her not be known only by the Levite who himself disowned her when he thrust her out to be assaulted and repeatedly raped. Let us instead call her Zacharel, which means "God remembers."

Zacharel suffered terribly in both life and death. But as incredible as it may seem, her story only ushered in more suffering and more violence. Judges 20 tells how the Benjaminites refused to accept responsibility for her death and instead began to war against the rest of Israel. After the tribes were again at peace, Judges 21 tells how the Israelites refused to let their daughters marry the Benjaminites; instead, they took young women from the town of Jabesh-gilead by force, and when they needed still more women, they encouraged the Benjaminites to kidnap young women from Shiloh and force them into marriage.

From Zacharel's torture and death to the kidnapping of the young women at Shiloh, the message of Judges 19-21 seems to be that the world is unsafe. A woman cannot expect protection from her father or her partner, her government or her God. A woman is not safe in her own home or in the home of a stranger, in a town or in the countryside.

This ancient message gains particular force as we consider women's reality in our own day. Women are still beaten, raped, and murdered. Women still suffer at the hands of strangers and at the hands of their own fathers and partners. Governments still respond inappropriately and inadequately. Even the church remains silent for the most part, and God seems absent.

Zacharel's story, however, encourages us to be aware of women's suffering, to talk about it, to speak out against it. Her story proper ends with that challenge: "Consider it, take counsel, and speak out" (v. 30). The Israelites tried to do that in their own way, but they only succeeded in multiplying the violence and inflicting further suffering. Today we need to try again.

We who have experienced assault and abuse still bear the physical and emotional scars. We need to consider our past, to work through our emotions and our insecurities. We need to speak out against our false feelings of shame and our low self-esteem. As we are able, we may even need to confront our former abusers with their responsibility.

We who currently live with abusive partners long to break the cycle of violence and transform our relationships. We need to consider our own needs and the needs of our children. We need to speak out to end our isolation. We may even need to remove ourselves from a dangerous home.

Even we who have been spared physical abuse cannot remain silent. We still hear the cries of other women. We need to join them in taking a stand against so-called domestic violence and other forms of abuse. With our prayers and with our practical assistance, we need to support them in their struggle.

None of us can afford to ignore the violence against women that continues in our own time. Zacharel's story is our own. Think about it, talk together about it, speak out against it.

Meditation Focus: How has your life been touched by physical abuse? How will you speak out against it?

Prayer: O God, today we remember all the unnamed women around the world who suffer physical abuse from their husbands or other family members, from soldiers or other strangers. Give them a clear vision of your love and respect for them. Help them build a network of supportive people to assist them in their struggle, and lead them out of suffering to a place of safety. In the name of Jesus, who also experienced physical abuse on this earth. Amen.

A Circle of Women

Scripture Reading: Ruth 4:13-17

The book of Ruth belongs to women in a special way. The widowed Naomi and her daughter-in-law Ruth occupy the spotlight for most of the book as its central characters. Naomi's other daughter-in-law, Orpah, plays an early supporting role. Women's work and women's relationships run through the whole book as prominent themes.

In addition, a circle of unnamed women of Bethlehem appears at two crucial points in the story. Near the beginning of the book, these unnamed women welcome Naomi back to Bethlehem. Near the end of the book, they help to celebrate the birth of her grandson. Like a Greek chorus in an ancient play, the group marks these two transition points in the story.

In the first case, the women speak on behalf of all the townspeople, voicing their surprise at Naomi's return (1:19). Could this really be Naomi, the women wondered. She had left Bethlehem years ago with her husband and two sons. Now she returned with only a Moabite daughter-in-law. She had left Bethlehem to seek a better life in Moab; now she was destitute and back at home.

Naomi did not hesitate to tell her troubles to the women of Bethlehem (1:20, 21). She told them how her life had changed. She spoke freely of her grief and of her complaint against God for all that had happened. And the women listened.

After this beginning, the unnamed women of Bethlehem fade into the background of the story. During the barley and wheat harvests, some of them must have worked beside Ruth in Boaz's fields. Others must have seen Naomi and Ruth at the well or passed them on the street. But not until the end of the story do the unnamed women speak again.

Once more, they mark an important transition in Naomi's life. As they shared her grief when she first returned to Bethlehem, now they shared her joy at the birth of her grandson. They praised God for restoring Naomi's family in this way. They admired the new baby and spoke well of Naomi's daughter-in-law. They even took part in naming the child.

With this ending, the book of Ruth comes full circle. At the beginning of the story, the women surrounded and supported Naomi in her grief. At the end, they surrounded her and shared her joy. The women's presence at these two points of the book serve to bracket the whole story, to encircle the entire narrative with a sense of community.

Today, we too are surrounded by a community of women. Our circle might include our mothers and grandmothers, sisters, cousins, aunts, friends, neighbors. Sometimes this circle meets in an almost formal fashion. We gather for wedding and baby showers. We meet as sewing circles and Bible study groups, as fellowship groups and support groups of various kinds. At other times, this circle functions much more informally. We may share a lunch hour or a coffee break. We may reach out to one another with a telephone call or a letter.

Formally and informally, women help us mark the transitions in our lives. Together we mourn the deaths in our families. Together we celebrate new beginnings. In times of joy, we can praise God together. In deep grief, we can even share our anger at God.

Like Naomi, sometimes we stand at the center of our circle. We need to know that others love and support us. We need to draw on their strength and rest in their care. But like the unnamed women of Bethlehem, sometimes we need to surround someone else with our love and compassion. We need to set aside our own concerns and give someone else our attention. In this circle of give and take, God provides the sustaining power. It is God who calls us together to be a community. It is God who grants us wisdom to know when to be silent with one another and when to speak. "Blessed be the Lord" (v. 14), said the unnamed women of Bethlehem. Blessed be the Lord.

Meditation Focus: Think of the many women in your own life. When have these women listened to you, comforted you, celebrated with you? When have you encircled them with compassion and joy?

Prayer: *Blessed Lord, we remember now the many women who have shared our lives. Thank you for the love that we have received from them. Thank you for the opportunity we have to love them in return. In the name of Jesus, who fills us and encircles us with your Spirit. Amen.*

Glory to God

Scripture Reading: 1 Samuel 4:19-22

The women attending Phinehas' wife knew that she was dying, but they tried to comfort her with the news that she had given birth to a son. After all, having a son was supposed to be the great dream of every Israelite woman; it was supposed to be the mark of her success and the fulfillment of her life. Yet in spite of the importance of sons in Old Testament culture, in spite of the importance of carrying on one's family line, Ichabod's mother was not comforted by the birth of her son. She breathed no prayer of thanks and gave no sigh of relief. She only called her child Ichabod, which means "the glory has departed."

According to the narrator, Phinehas' wife called her son Ichabod because the ark of God had been captured and because of her father-in-law and her husband (v. 21). It is easy to see how the child's name might be related to the loss of the ark of God, for the ark was the chief symbol of God's presence and glory among the people of Israel. But to understand how the loss of God's glory was related to Eli and Phinehas, we need to understand their priestly ministry in Israel.

In 1 Samuel 2, Eli was already an old man, and we learn that his two sons, Phinehas and Hophni, were serving as priests at Shiloh. But instead of faithfully carrying out their responsibilities, the two men abused their positions as priests. When the people came to sacrifice, Phinehas and Hophni took the best part of the meat for themselves instead of burning it before the Lord. They had sexual relations with the women who also ministered at Shiloh. And Eli's protest did not stop them.

Now the people of Israel had been talking about the sins of the priests (2:23,24). So even if Phinehas had said nothing about his activities, Phinehas' wife would probably have known the truth. The priesthood—represented by her father-in-law and her husband—had already caused God's glory to suffer. The Philistines had simply delivered the final blow. The ark of the covenant had been captured and taken away from Israel.

To Ichabod's mother, nothing mattered more than God's glory. She did not speak of the deaths of Phinehas and Eli. She did not express joy over the birth of her son. She did not even appear concerned for her own life. God's glory had departed from Israel; that was all that mattered.

This snapshot of Ichabod's mother has much to teach us about setting our own priorities today. Like her, we too live in a society which promotes certain values. While her society emphasized the importance of children, our society seems to emphasize material prosperity. Our country may stress military security. Our friends and family may focus on having children and spending time together. But Ichabod's mother points us toward God as the chief priority in life.

In the sermon on the mount, Jesus teaches us the very same lesson about priorities. "For where your treasure is, there your heart will be also" (Matt. 6:21). "You cannot serve God and wealth" (Matt. 6:24). "But strive first for the kingdom of God and his righteousness, and all these things will be given to you as well" (Matt. 6:33).

When we put God's presence and glory first, then everything else falls into place. We are set free to work not just for money or for self-esteem or for power, but for God's glory. We are set free to be with our friends and family not just on our own terms and to satisfy our own desires, but for their good and for God's glory.

Without a concern for God's presence and glory, we cannot hope to live faithfully before God. So like Ichabod's mother, may we also be sensitive to God's presence. In life and at the end of life, may we also think first of God's glory.

Meditation Focus: For the Israelites, the ark was the symbol of God's presence and glory. What signs of God's presence and glory have we been given today? How can we express God's glory by the way we live?

Prayer: O God, we confess that we have too often sought our own glory instead of yours. Forgive us for keeping the best things for ourselves, for robbing you of what is rightfully yours, for using other people to satisfy our own desires. Give us a heart to love and serve you. For yours is the power and the glory. Amen.

Not Only a Witch

Scripture Reading: 1 Samuel 28:3–25

If we remember her at all, most of us remember the woman of Endor as the witch of Endor. We read her story against the background of the Mosaic law which declared anyone who consulted spirits "abhorrent" to God (Deut. 18:9-14). We think of her as one of the mediums that Saul had unsuccessfully tried to ban from Israel, but who nevertheless continued to practice her art in secret.

But there is more to the woman of Endor than this unorthodox and outlawed spirituality. In fact, Saul's unnamed servants who also appear in this story would probably have remembered her more as a compassionate woman than as a witch. It is this less well-remembered and more compassionate side of her story that concerns us here.

The woman had compassion on Saul not once, but three times during Saul's visit to her home. Her first demonstration of compassion came with her initial willingness to contact a spirit for Saul. Even though Saul was a stranger to her, and even though she knew that contacting the dead was a crime, she agreed to help him. For this desperate stranger at her door, she was even willing to risk her life.

Once the woman realized that her petitioner was Saul, she still continued to help him. At that point she could have simply sent Samuel back without a word. After all, since the king had outlawed her magic, she hardly owed him her continued cooperation. But instead, she allowed the two men to meet. As Saul would later tell Samuel, the king was desperate: God would not answer him, and Samuel was dead. The woman was his only hope, and she chose to have compassion on him.

After Samuel had returned to his resting place, the woman again had compassion on the terrified king. She urged him to eat and to strengthen himself for the ordeal ahead of him. The "morsel of bread" (v. 22) that she offered him was the best she had: a fatted calf and fresh baked bread.

The woman of Endor had compassion for Saul even though he had never had any compassion for her. He had taken away her freedom of worship and threatened her life. But instead of taking her revenge, the woman helped him make contact with Samuel, did not refuse him even once she knew his true identity, and offered food and drink to him as a guest under her roof.

For the narrator, the woman of Endor was not a one-dimensional character, but a whole person. She was not only a witch, but a woman; not only a medium who communicated with the dead, but a living human being who had compassion on a broken man. The narrator presents her not as a stereotypical, cardboard character, but as a real person.

In our own perception of others, we are not always so generous. We remember the woman of Endor only as the witch of Endor. We label others as saints or sinners, desirable or undesirable, often on the basis of a single trait. That kind of pigeonhole thinking may be convenient, but it is not as honest as it could be: it makes others appear much more one-dimensional than they really are.

At other times, when we are on the receiving end, such one-dimensional thinking can make us appear much more one-dimensional than we really are. If we talk about women in the Bible, then we are labelled as feminists. If we question established traditions, then we are remembered as troublemakers. Like the woman of Endor, we are too quickly reduced to a caricature, too easily labelled and misunderstood by others.

But the truth is that we are saints and sinners, people with desirable and undesirable characteristics. Like the woman of Endor, sometimes we may act like witches and lawbreakers, at other times like people of compassion. No stereotype can explain us, no cardboard figure can take our place. We are real people—multi-dimensional people—on a journey to wholeness as God's unique creation.

Meditation Focus: How do you tend to stereotype other people? How do people tend to stereotype you? How does that one-dimensional thinking affect your relationships with others?

Prayer: O God, like the woman of Endor, we too live fractured lives. We are a curious mixture of good and bad, of faithfulness and unfaithfulness. Help us to become more nearly the people you would have us be. In the name of Jesus, who died and rose again to make us whole and holy people. Amen.

Politics and Peacemaking

Scripture Reading: 2 Samuel 14:1-22

What kind of woman was the unnamed woman from Tekoa? Neither Joab nor David addressed her by any name or title. The woman only referred to herself as the king's servant. The narrator only spoke of her as a wise woman. But today we might call her a lobbyist, for she sought to influence government in the direction of certain political interests.

Like the contemporary political lobbyist, this woman acted as a representative for someone else. She did not act alone, but on behalf of Joab, the commander of King David's army. She received Joab's instructions about what strategy to use, what to say, even what to wear.

At the same time, however, the woman was not simply Joab's mouthpiece. Joab may have told her what to say, but once she stood before the king, she was really on her own. Like the contemporary lobbyist, she had to use her own judgment and skill, her own diplomacy and persuasive power.

But there the similarity between the woman of Tekoa and the contemporary lobbyist ends, for unlike her contemporary counterpart, this woman had no professional standing. She was from the small town of Tekoa, outside of the circle of power in Jerusalem. She was a stranger to the court, a woman in a setting dominated by men, a commoner meeting royalty.

In addition, unlike the contemporary lobbyist, this woman had no political power of her own. She had no voting power, no media coverage, no political leverage. In the political life of ancient Israel, the king held all the power to banish or to bless, to kill or to preserve life; the woman's only power lay in her persuasive words.

And yet in spite of her political disadvantage, the woman from Tekoa took the risk of approaching King David. Why did she agree to Joab's request? Why did she bother involving herself in the political intrigue of the royal court? Why did she take the risk of confronting the king with his mistake?

Part of the answer to these questions seems to be implied in the woman's own question to the king. She asked him, "Why then have you planned such a thing against the people of God?"

(v. 13). With these words, the woman made her appeal on behalf of all the people. She was not simply working for Joab, but for the whole people of God. She knew that David's unwillingness to forgive Absalom not only made the king unhappy, but threatened the whole kingdom as well. And so she had agreed to Joab's plan to be a peacemaker between David and his son Absalom.

Today we also face serious political situations that threaten our world. There is still violence and injustice at home and abroad, economic oppression, human rights abuses, environmental dangers. There is need for peacemaking today just as much as there was a need in the time of the woman from Tekoa.

Sometimes we may try to ignore the troubles of the world by focusing on our own immediate circle of family and friends. Like the woman from Tekoa, we may be far removed from the political arena, and we may want to keep it that way. We may refuse to believe that political affairs have anything to do with us. We may refuse to get involved.

Yet as citizens of our countries and citizens of the kingdom of God, we too have a responsibility to work for peace and justice in our own world as God leads us. We may not all be Joabs with political influence and ability. We may not all be wise women with the gift of speaking in public. But we too must do what we can.

For some of us that may mean writing letters or joining a political group. For others that may mean addressing problems more directly through mission or service work. For still others that may even mean entering the circles of government as the wise woman from Tekoa entered the king's court. For all of us that will mean much prayer and dependence on God.

Meditation Focus: Think of a specific social or community need. How could you help to be part of the solution instead of part of the problem?

Prayer: Sovereign God, forgive us our indifference to the serious political situations of our day. Shake us out of our complacency. Help us to be part of the solution instead of part of the problem, to be active peacemakers instead of passive bystanders. In the name of Jesus, who is our peace. Amen.

Wisdom

Scripture Reading: 2 Samuel 20:14-22

For most of us, reading these nine verses from 2 Samuel is probably as bewildering as watching only the second act of a three-act play. We are unfamiliar with the setting, the plot, and the characters. We enter the story in the middle of the action, unaware of all the events leading up to the scene before us. And so to understand this story of the wise woman of Abel, we need a few additional details.

The time is late in King David's reign over Judah and Israel. The setting is the city of Abel, a walled city in the northern tip of Israelite territory. The plot centers around the rebellion of certain Israelites against David's kingship. The cast of characters includes Joab, David's army commander, who has been ordered to hunt down the leader of the rebellion; Sheba, the leader of the rebellion, who hopes to overthrow David as king; and an unnamed wise woman, who is perhaps a judge or some other official in the city of Abel.

This wise woman clearly had the authority and trust of her people. She had the authority both to initiate and to conclude negotiations with Joab on their behalf. Her people trusted her judgment and agreed with her decision to execute Sheba as a traitor.

But the woman also commanded a measure of respect and trust outside of the city as well. At her word, Joab's men summoned Joab to the wall to speak with her. Joab himself accepted her authority to negotiate with him and trusted her to carry out the terms of their agreement.

This woman knew how to use her position of authority and trust wisely. She did not rouse her people to respond in kind with military action. Instead, her first step was to open negotiations with Joab and his men who had laid siege to the city. She chose to answer Joab's battering ram with the persuasive voice of reason. Her wisdom was first of all peaceable.

In addition, her wisdom was humble. With great diplomacy, she addressed her words to Joab as the words of "your servant" (v. 17). She did not accuse him directly, but first set the stage for her appeal by talking about Abel's history as part of God's heritage. Only after that did she charge Joab with destroying the city, and even then her accusation took the form of a question: "Why will you swallow up the heritage of the Lord?" (v. 19).

With this question, the woman showed that her wisdom was also God-centered. She remained focused on the larger issue of preserving David's kingdom as God's heritage. In contrast, Joab's haste to capture Sheba had made him forget why he needed to stop Sheba's rebellion in the first place: it was all because Sheba wanted to destroy the kingdom. Now the woman's pointed question made Joab realize that he himself was about to destroy part of the very kingdom he wanted to protect.

Finally, the woman's wisdom took into account both the needs of the city and the needs of Joab. She was not so biased toward the city that she ignored Joab's desires. But neither was she so eager to please Joab that she compromised the integrity of the city in his favor. Joab wanted Sheba released to him, but the woman knew that the city needed to retain its place in God's heritage as a center of wisdom and as a loyal part of David's kingdom. She knew it must take its own action against a traitor like Sheba, and so she countered Joab's request with a better alternative: the city of Abel would judge Sheba.

In her negotiations with Joab, the woman of Abel offers us a model of wisdom that is peaceable, humble, diplomatic, God-centered, and well-balanced. That is the same wisdom we need as we face the challenges of our own day. We too need to know how to meet violence with peace, how to treat others with respect without compromising ourselves, how to remain faithful to God's will.

As leaders who hold positions of authority and trust in our own communities, corporations, governments, churches, and other organizations, let us follow the example of the wise woman of Abel. As those responsible for choosing such leaders, let us seek God's guidance and choose wisely.

Meditation Focus: In your own life, where do you need the wisdom of the woman of Abel? What role models of wisdom do you see among the leaders in the church and the world today?

Prayer: O God of wisdom, help us to see clearly the issues we face in our own lives, to act humbly and with integrity, and to hold fast to the good. Amen.

Conflict and Compassion

Scripture Reading: 1 Kings 3:16–28

Solomon had a difficult case before him: no witnesses besides the two plaintiffs, no evidence besides their two very different testimonies. But God had promised Solomon wisdom, and Solomon relied on that promise now. He listened to the two women, weighed their two stories, and devised a plan that would reveal the truth. Solomon made a wise decision in a difficult situation, and all Israel was impressed with his judgment.

But Solomon's part in the story was actually relatively easy compared to that of the two women. As king and judge, Solomon was ultimately detached from the scene before him. Unlike the two women, he had no vested interest in its outcome. He did not experience their conflict. He did not share their strong emotions. So Solomon's example may teach us something about making wise decisions in relatively calm situations, but it tells us little about the more difficult task of making wise decisions in the midst of conflict. For that, we need to turn to the example of the two women.

Their story began long before the two women came to King Solomon. They had shared the same house, the same profession, the same experience of anticipating motherhood. They had given birth to sons within days of one another. With all that they had in common, they should have been the best of friends; instead, they stood before the king as opponents.

The first woman to speak to the king told him what had gone wrong. One night, the other woman had accidentally smothered her son in bed. Then, after discovering what she had done, that woman had traded her dead baby for the first woman's living son. In the morning, the first woman was shocked to discover that the infant in her arms was dead and was not hers at all.

Before the first woman had even finished her side of the story, the second woman also began to speak. She claimed that the first woman's son had been the one to die and that her son was the living one. Soon the two women were arguing back and forth as if they were not before the king and his court, but back in their own house. Even when the king called for a sword to divide the infant boy in two, the women could not agree with one another. One of the women begged the king to let the infant live; the other dared the king to divide it.

The harsh reaction of the one woman makes the whole story even more incredible than it has been up to this point. Even if we take into account our more sentimental attitude toward children, the woman's response remains inconceivable. How could anyone demand the death of another person whose only crime was being alive?

Perhaps the woman guessed correctly that the king would never carry out the grisly deed and simply tried to force him to admit it. Or perhaps she got carried away with her own argument and immediately regretted her thoughtless words. But at that moment in the midst of the conflict, she chose self-interest. She did not spare the feelings of her former friend and housemate. She did not seem to care that her words endangered the life of a little boy.

The other woman, however, responded with compassion for the child. Perhaps she really was its true mother, as Solomon and the story's narrator assume. Or perhaps it was her son that was dead, and she could not bear to see another young life end. Even in the midst of conflict, the welfare of the child remained uppermost in her mind. She would rather let the other woman raise the child as her own than see him dead.

The conflicts we face in our own households and work places are seldom as extreme as the conflict faced by these two women. Yet time and again, we also must choose between self-interest and compassion for others, between a response that disregards other people and a response that cares for them. May we choose wisely even under pressure, as the compassionate woman chose wisely even in the midst of conflict.

Meditation Focus: Think of a conflict you have had with another person. How did you resolve it?

Prayer: *O God, as we experience various conflicts in our lives, we pray that we might face them with a spirit of compassion for other people. Make us sensitive to your leading and responsive to the needs of others. In the name of Jesus, who had compassion even for prostitutes and others outside of the social and religious mainstream. Amen.*

The Word of the Lord

Scripture Reading: 1 Kings 17:8-16

The key to understanding the story of Elijah and the widow of Zarephath appears to be "the word of the Lord." The phrase first occurs at the beginning of the story (v. 8), where God tells Elijah to go to Zarephath to a widow who will feed him. Then at the end of the story, "the word of the Lord" occurs again, this time in the narrator's comments on the faithfulness of God's word to and through Elijah (v. 16). Bracketed by these two instances of the same phrase, the story of Elijah and the widow of Zarephath demonstrates "the word of the Lord" in action. God's word is faithful.

So far, so good. But what is often overlooked in this story is that the word of the Lord does not come only to Elijah. A careful reading of the passage reveals a surprising detail: the word of the Lord had also come to the widow of Zarephath. In verse 9, the narrator records God's own words: "for I have commanded a widow there to feed you." No wonder the woman willingly brings water to Elijah and even bakes him a cake before she makes one for herself and for her son. God had spoken to her, prepared her, moved her to feed the prophet of Israel.

And so in the midst of a story about the faithfulness of God's word to the prophet Elijah, we also find that God's word came to the widow of Zarephath, a poor, unnamed, Canaanite woman. This detail of the story illustrates several truths about God's word.

First of all, God's word transcends geographical boundaries. It may come to Jerusalem and to Zarephath, to places we call holy and to places we do not. As the word of God came in all its clarity and power to the poor widow in Zarephath, so it may come to us wherever we may be: in North America or in Asia, in the rural areas or in the cities, at home or at work, in the sanctuary or in the kitchen. God's word cannot be contained by physical limits.

Second, God's word reaches the poor. In this story, for example, God's word came to a widow, one of the poorest of the poor in ancient Israel. In his earthly ministry, Jesus preached good news to the poor—to widows, beggars, and prostitutes. Even today the word of God may also come to the poor and hungry of our world. God's word is not limited by economic status.

Third, God's word comes to ordinary people of faith. It is not only for prophets, priests, and other religious leaders. As God's word came both to Elijah and to the widow of Zarephath, so the word of God continues to come both to those who work in the church and to those who work in the home and in the world. God's word is not tied to official religious hierarchies, but honors faith.

Finally, the word of God breaks through ethnic and cultural barriers. The widow of Zarephath was not an Israelite, and yet God spoke to her and used her to provide for Israel's prophet. In the New Testament church, the word of God came to both Hebrews and Greeks, to both Jews and Gentiles. To this day the word of God is not limited by family background or culture or race. God's word is for all people.

In short, God's word knows no geographical, economic, institutional, or cultural boundaries. Humanly speaking, it comes even to the most unlikely places and even to the most unlikely people. And so the word of God may even come to us.

Like the widow of Zarephath, we too may live quietly, away from the official centers of religious life and power, occupied with the daily work of making a living and caring for our households. We too may be unnamed and ordinary women, poor or ethnic minority women. And yet we too may receive the word of the Lord, for God is faithful. Speak, Lord, your servants hear.

Meditation Focus: In what ways have you received "the word of the Lord"? How has that word been active in your own life?

Prayer: *O God, we thank you for your word that comes to us through Bible reading and prayer, through the events of our lives and our relationships with other people. Like the widow of Zarephath, may we be sensitive to your voice and obedient to your leading. In the name of Jesus, the Living Word. Amen.*

Making a Miracle

Scripture Reading: 2 Kings 4:1-7

How does God make a miracle? In the beginning, God spoke and created the miracle of life. In the gospels, Jesus spoke and healed the sick and the demon-possessed. In Acts, the Spirit of God descended in a mighty wind and spoke through the disciples in many different languages. In these and other instances, God performed a miracle with a divine word.

But the Scriptures also show us that sometimes God chooses to work a miracle using the more ordinary objects and actions of human life. For example, when Jesus fed the crowds, he did so with the ordinary loaves and fishes of a little boy's lunch. When he gave sight to a man born blind, he began by spreading ordinary mud on the man's eyes. And here in this story of a prophet's widow, God also used ordinary means for extraordinary results.

The word of the prophet Elisha may have set events in motion, but then the rest was left to the neighbors who lent their jars, to the children who carried them, and to the unnamed woman who poured the oil. For this miracle, God used ordinary oil, ordinary household jars, and ordinary people.

If the neighbors had refused to lend their vessels, God could not have filled them. If the woman had borrowed only a few vessels, then God could have filled only those few. God chose to limit the divine power and to depend instead on human compassion and human action. Once there were no more empty vessels, there was also no more oil.

Today we too could use a miracle. As Elisha heard the cry of the prophet's widow, so we too hear the cries of the poor in our own world. As the prophet's widow suffered from poverty and an oppressive economic system, so people still endure the same trials today. People still go hungry. Poverty still threatens the well-being and freedom of many unnamed women and their families.

In the light of such human need, we might well ask, If God is a God of miracles, where is our miracle today? How can we believe in God's mercy and miraculous power, when so many people still suffer and starve? Such questions nag us and make us suspicious of any talk of miracles.

And so we try to re-interpret this widow's story to suit the reality of our world and the skepticism of our souls. We say that God satisfies our spiritual hunger and thirst. When we are lonely or confused, God reaches out to touch us. When we need forgiveness and acceptance, God loves us. We read this story as a lesson of divine love and provision for human spiritual and emotional need.

But while it is true that God meets our inner and hidden needs, this story of the prophet's widow seems to say something more: God meets our outward physical needs as well. The Merciful One did not simply comfort the widow in her mourning or give her strength to mother her children. The Sovereign God did not simply lead her to reach out to Elisha and to her neighbors for assistance. Instead, the Merciful and Sovereign God intervened in the widow's poverty-stricken situation and worked through her and others to provide for her material needs.

Today God is still the same, still caring for the poor and still longing to answer their cries. But God also continues to limit the divine intervention and power to work through ordinary means and through ordinary people. The Merciful and Sovereign God invites our participation in the divine work of meeting human need.

Like this unnamed widow, her children, and neighbors, we too can cooperate with God's work in the world. We can work at bridging the gap between the haves and the have-nots of our world. We can begin to work with the poor by sharing our resources, our vessels. We can take what little we have and start pouring it out. And then perhaps God will use us to make a miracle.

Meditation Focus: In what specific ways can you cooperate with God's work in the world to alleviate poverty? In what ways do you stand in the way of God's work?

Prayer: Merciful and Sovereign God, grant us the courage to reach out to one another, to share what we have, to work together against the suffering in this world. Fill our empty vessels, multiply our meager resources, and transform our ordinary actions with your extraordinary power. Amen.

Great Giving

Scripture Reading: 2 Kings 4:8-17

In the ancient world, hospitality was one of the chief virtues, and refusing hospitality one of the chief sins. The lack of hospitality on the part of Sodom contributed to the destruction of that city (Ezek. 16:49). The lack of hospitality given to a woman in Gibeah led to her death and eventually to civil war (Judg. 19-20). Here in our Scripture reading, the hospitality of the woman of Shunem is rewarded with the gift of a son.

As a host, the Shunammite woman excelled in hospitality. She did not simply invite Elisha for a meal, but "urged" him to stop at her home. She invited him repeatedly, until he became a regular guest at her table. She even decided to make a separate guest room for him, so that he would have not only a place to eat, but also a place to stay whenever he passed by. The Shunammite woman did everything she could to provide for Elisha's needs.

Many English translations call this woman a "wealthy" woman, but the word in Hebrew may also be translated "great," which might imply the woman's high standing in her community. In fact, the story gives evidence of both the woman's wealth and her social position. As a wealthy woman, the Shunammite had a large enough house and sufficient funds to make an extra guest room on the roof of her house. As a great woman, she was apparently part of a powerful and well-connected family, for she could easily refuse Elisha's offer to speak to the king or to the commander of the army on her behalf.

This woman was also great in her own household. She took the initiative in inviting Elisha to eat in her home. And although she spoke with her husband about making a room for Elisha, it was she who first had the idea and who planned the prophet's room. She was no figurehead, no silent partner to her husband, but truly the mistress of her household.

This woman used her wealth, her position in her household, and her reputation in her community to provide for Elisha. Even more importantly, she provided for him generously and without expecting anything in return. She did not expect Elisha to pay for his food or lodging. She refused his offer of political or military consideration. She even protested Elisha's promise of a son. Her giving was as great as her wealth.

Like the Shunammite woman, we also may be great and wealthy people in some ways. We too may have the resources to feed those of our own household and still provide for strangers. We may have the resources to shelter our own household and still provide shelter for others. We may be rich in education, physical strength, mental and emotional health, political power, and spiritual resources.

Sometimes we may be tempted to restrict those resources to ourselves and to our own families. We are tempted to be generous with ourselves and tight-fisted with others. We forget that God welcomed us when we were strangers, fed us when we were hungry, sheltered us when we had nowhere else to go.

At other times we may give—but with the hope of getting something in return. We expect others to thank us and God to bless us. We give in order to get. We tithe in order to secure yet more riches for ourselves. We are attracted by the gospel of prosperity instead of the gospel of Jesus.

It is true that giving sometimes results in getting. Even the Shunammite is blessed with a son at the end of our Scripture reading. But she did not give in order to get. In fact, it was in spite of her protests that Elisha and Gehazi decided that she should have a son. The woman herself seemed content to give without gain.

In her provision for Elisha, the Shunammite woman demonstrated true giving and true hospitality. Be kind to strangers. Feed the hungry. Shelter the weary. Give generously without expecting anything in return. As the apostle Paul would later quote Jesus, "It is more blessed to give than to receive" (Acts 20:35b).

Meditation Focus: In what ways are you powerful and wealthy? How can you use your resources in the service of other people?

Prayer: O God, we thank you for the example of the woman of Shunem, who did what she could to serve the prophet Elisha. Like her, may we also be sensitive to the needs of others and share what we have with them. In the name of Jesus, who gave himself for us. Amen.

Loving Our Enemies

Scripture Reading: 2 Kings 5:1-19

Our story begins and ends with Naaman, the proud and successful commander of the Aramean army. At the beginning of the story, he has leprosy or some other skin disease; at the end, he is cured. At the beginning of the story, he is thoroughly Aramean; at the end, he recognizes the God of Israel.

But Naaman's story would have had no happy ending without the quiet involvement of two unnamed women in his household. The more socially prominent woman was Naaman's wife, who shared his high status in Aramean society. The other woman was perhaps no more than a child—a young Hebrew girl who served Naaman's wife as a personal servant. The servant girl plays such a small part in this short story of Naaman's healing, that she might easily be overlooked. But as the one who started the whole chain of events that led to Naaman's healing, she is worth our close attention.

This girl was a Hebrew, captured by the Arameans in one of their many raids against Israel. The Hebrew text describes her with a term that usually describes an unmarried woman. And since women generally married at twelve or thirteen years of age, this servant was likely but a child when she was taken from her homeland.

Perhaps some months or years had already passed since the Hebrew girl had first joined the Aramean household. The text does not give any indication how long she had been serving Naaman's wife. It gives no details about her responsibilities or experiences within the household. The text only reports one very brief conversation with her mistress. But from those few words, we learn two important personal details about her.

First of all, the servant had retained her faith in the God of Israel and in God's prophet Elisha. Even though God had allowed her to be captured and forced into servitude in a foreign land, she resisted the temptation to turn her back on God. Although she was surrounded by Arameans who worshipped Rimmon and many other deities, she kept her faith in the one true God of Israel.

Second, the Hebrew servant had a good working relationship with Naaman's wife. She cared enough about her mistress to express a concern for Naaman that seemed quite natural and sincere. And Naaman's wife trusted her servant enough to tell her husband about their conversation.

The servant's genuine care for her mistress was truly remarkable given the context of their relationship. Servant and mistress were at opposite ends of the social spectrum. They had different religions. They were from two different nations that were periodically at war with one another. The Hebrew girl had been captured and forced into her position as a servant. She had every reason to hate her mistress.

Instead, this young Hebrew servant gives us an Old Testament example of Jesus' New Testament command to love our enemies (Matt. 5:43-48; Luke 6:27-36). Her Aramean mistress was her natural enemy, but she served her without complaint and with genuine concern. She actively sought the good of her enemy. And she did so without compromising her own faith.

In our own day, economic, ethnic, religious, and personality differences still divide people from one another. Our friends tend to come from the same economic bracket as we do. Our churches divide far too often and too easily along ethnic lines. We tend to avoid people of other faiths. We are suspicious of people with abrasive or eccentric personalities.

Yet Jesus' command calls us to move beyond these differences to love those who are our "natural enemies." We need to go beyond a separate peace or a live-and-let-live neutrality. We need to do good to our enemies, to bless them, to pray for them, to share our faith with them.

Like this young Hebrew servant who served Naaman's wife, may we too learn to serve our enemies and to keep our faith in a hostile environment. May we bless those who mistreat us and thus set forth a chain of events that leads to healing.

Meditation Focus: Who would you define as your "natural enemy"? How could you carry out Jesus' command to love our enemies?

Prayer: *O God, we confess that we would rather ignore or avoid those people who differ from us, who are our natural enemies. Teach us instead to love them and to share our faith with them. In the name of Jesus Christ, who loved us while we were yet strangers, and who died for our sake. Amen.*

In Search of Truth

Scripture Reading: 2 Chronicles 9:1-12

Historians suggest that the main reason for the Queen of Sheba's visit to Jerusalem may have been the negotiation of a trade agreement between Israel and Sheba. After all, the Old Testament speaks elsewhere about the Sabaeans as traders (e.g., Isa. 60:6; Ezek. 27:22), and Solomon and the Queen of Sheba do exchange a variety of goods during the course of their meeting. But the Chronicler emphasizes a different aspect of this royal visit: the demonstration of Solomon's wisdom and wealth.

News of Solomon's wise judgment and prosperity had spread from Jerusalem to all of Israel, to Edom, to Arabia, and even to Sheba, over a thousand miles south of Jerusalem. The Queen of Sheba had heard enough rumors and reports to arouse her curiosity about King Solomon. Was he really as wise as she had heard? Was he really so wealthy? The Queen decided to discover the truth for herself by making the long trip north.

The Queen of Sheba was well qualified to judge Solomon's abilities. She herself must have been wise, for she had many things to discuss with Solomon and many difficult questions for him to answer. She herself was obviously wealthy, for she travelled with a large caravan of camels and servants, and she brought Solomon expensive gifts of spices, gold, and precious stones.

At the end of her journey, the Queen was not disappointed. Solomon displayed his wisdom by answering all her questions. He displayed his wealth in his house and furnishings, in his fine food and hospitality, in his officials and servants, and even in his temple and burnt offerings. Finally the Queen had to admit that the reports she had heard had told only part of the truth; Solomon was far wiser and far wealthier than she had imagined.

We might have expected the Queen to have been favorably impressed with Solomon's keen insight and riches. But her words in praise of the God of Israel (v. 8) might well have taken us by surprise. As a Sabaean, the Queen of Sheba worshipped her own gods of the sun, moon, and stars. She was a foreigner, a stranger to Israelite religion. Yet here in response to Solomon's greatness, she gave praise to God.

The Queen of Sheba was a positive example of a woman in search of truth. She was not content with ordinary rumors or official reports or other second-hand information. Instead, she conducted her own investigation at considerable expense and effort. She presented her hard questions. She examined the evidence. And when she discovered the truth, she praised God.

Jesus himself used the story of the Queen of Sheba as a positive example to answer some of the Jews who did not accept his teaching (Matt. 12:38-42; Luke 11:29-32). As the Queen of Sheba had come from far away to listen to Solomon, so these Jews should have listened to Jesus. As the Queen of Sheba had recognized Solomon's wisdom and wealth, so these Jews should have recognized Jesus' teaching and miraculous works. The greatness of Jesus surpassed the greatness of Solomon. And the faith of the Queen of Sheba surpassed the faith of the Jews who rejected Jesus.

Today we too have the opportunity to search for truth, to investigate the wisdom and wealth of God in Jesus Christ. In its own way, our search may be as long and as costly as the Queen of Sheba's. We cannot rely on second-hand reports, but must spend our own personal time and energy in searching out the truth. We must make the long journey in prayer, in worship, in study, in service, in relationship with other pilgrims, until we too are satisfied.

Like the Queen of Sheba, let us bring our hard questions of theology, ethics, and personal experience. Let us examine all the evidence and see for ourselves the wisdom and riches of God in Jesus Christ. And finally may we praise God with the apostle Paul: "O the depth of the riches and wisdom and knowledge of God!" (Rom. 11:33a).

Meditation Focus: In what ways have you experienced the wisdom and riches of God? What part has prayer, worship, Bible study, service, and community played in those experiences?

Prayer: O God, we long for the truth that will set us free to worship you. Give us a teachable spirit that we might hear and accept your wisdom. Open our eyes that we might see the riches of your grace. In the name of the One who is greater than Solomon. Amen.

Honest Anger

Scripture Reading: Job 2:1-10

If anyone suffered as much as Job, it was Job's wife. Together, the two had lost all of their livestock and most of their servants. Together, they mourned their sons and daughters, who had perished in a hurricane. But finally, even that togetherness in suffering was taken away from them. Job's affliction of boils drove him to the city ash heap where he did nothing but sit and scrape himself with a piece of pottery. Job's wife was left to bear her grief alone and to care for Job as best she could.

Jewish legend says that the once wealthy woman became a water carrier to support Job and herself. But when her employer learned that she was Job's wife and that she was taking him bread, he refused to have her as a servant. Job's wife then had no choice but to sell her hair for food.

And so Job's wife suffered greatly. She had lost her livestock, her children, and her healthy husband. She was forced to support Job and herself in a society in which women had few options for employment. She experienced hunger and public humiliation.

Yet for all that, Job's wife did not dwell on her own problems. When she went out to see Job sitting on the ash heap, she did not think of herself; she thought only of Job and his suffering. Surely anything would be better than the torment he suffered. In compassion and despair over her husband, Job's wife cried out to him, "Curse God, and die" (v. 9).

Her words were not simply the words of the devil as Augustine, Calvin, and others have argued. These were desperate words, despairing, angry, and helpless words, uttered by one sufferer to another.

Yet for all their anger and despair, the words of Job's wife also remained curiously faithful. They acknowledged God's presence in human affairs and God's power to inflict human suffering and even to cause death. Angry but honest, these words expressed God's power at the same time they expressed the woman's powerlessness.

The New Testament tells us that even the demons believe in God (James 2:19), so perhaps we should not overrate the faithfulness of Job's wife. Yet in her position, many of us would have difficulty maintaining even that little bit of faith in God's power. Our response would more likely be one of disbelief and denial: if there is such suffering, then God is dead.

In fact, that response to deny God is the very temptation we face today. Like Job's wife, we too are touched by the suffering of others; on the ash heaps of our own world we see people who suffer hunger, poverty, disease, and a host of other ills that seem unreasonable and undeserved. Like Job's wife, we may also try to do the best we can to care for those who suffer: we may give money to the poor, visit the sick, support local and overseas work, limit our consumption, recycle our goods, pray for peace and justice. And yet human suffering continues, and at times we feel as helpless and as angry as Job's wife. We are tempted to doubt and to deny God's existence and power. We are tempted to turn away in despair and unbelief.

At such times, we need to remember Job's wife and her response to suffering. Like her, may we be sensitive to the suffering of others and yet retain our faith in God's existence and power. Like her, may we have the courage to take our anger and despair to God. And may God grant us the grace to be angry and sin not, and to move beyond our honest anger to honest praise.

Meditation Focus: Like Job's wife, the psalmists expressed their anger at God, but they were also able to move beyond their anger to praise (e.g., Ps. 13). When have you expressed anger to God? Could you move beyond your anger to praise?

Prayer: *Our God, we pray for those who suffer on the ash heaps of our world. We remember all those who have lost their livelihood, their families, and their health through war, through the injustice of governments and business interests, through lack of medical care, through lack of food and clean water, through floods and hurricanes and other natural disasters. Help us to identify with those who suffer, that we might work with them and for them to end the pain in your world. In the name of Jesus, who suffers and works with us. Amen.*

In the City Gates

Scripture Reading: Proverbs 31:10-31

The unnamed woman who ends the book of Proverbs appears to be the woman who has it all and who does it all. She has a supportive husband and grateful children. She is a capable household manager and a commercially successful buyer and seller of goods and property. She is generous, optimistic, wise, kind-hearted, and God-fearing. Her many activities and abilities make an impressive litany.

As the opening line of our passage suggests, such a biblical superwoman is indeed rare. In fact, the poem's own portrait is probably not any one woman, but a composite of many women and their various qualities and abilities. This is the ideal woman, likely intended as a man's guide for choosing a wife.

Yet even as a composite picture, even with its apparently exhaustive and exhausting list of accomplishments, this picture of ideal womanhood is far from complete. It tells us nothing about women's friendships or intellectual activities. It remains silent about women's religious responsibilities and political involvements. With these limitations, the poem stands squarely in the patriarchal tradition which viewed women primarily as wives and mothers and which interpreted their lives primarily in relation to their husbands.

The poem's point of view is limited further by its strict poetic structure. In the original Hebrew, the poem takes the form of an acrostic: the first line begins with the first letter of the Hebrew alphabet, and each successive line begins with the next letter until the alphabet is complete. Anything not expressed in this form would have been omitted, and so the poem is not as complete or as well organized as it might have been.

In spite of its patriarchal viewpoint and its strict poetic structure, however, the poem offers us an example of an industrious, capable, and relatively independent woman. In addition, the poem moves beyond a narrow patriarchal bias to affirm the woman's own worth and accomplishments. It supports her right to be adequately rewarded for her labor and justly praised for her work (v. 31).

Too often women have not been given this credit for their contributions. Even in biblical studies, women have too often been restricted or silenced or ignored. We hear much more about Elisha curing Naaman the leper than about the Hebrew maidservant who brought the two together. We read much more about Job's suffering than the suffering of his wife. We find it much easier to call Philip an evangelist than to grant the same title to the Samaritan woman who evangelized an entire town. And yet in the spirit of Proverbs, these women and many others deserve to be recognized and rewarded for their work.

As we recognize the contributions of these biblical women, we will also need to recognize their full humanity. The wife of Manoah was not simply a wife, but a woman of great faith. The unnamed wise women of Abel and Tekoa may have been married, but they appear in the biblical narrative instead as public and political figures, known in the city gates in their own right. Not all biblical women were married or functioned only as wives and mothers as Proverbs seems to assume.

Like their biblical counterparts, women today still perform valuable work both inside and outside of their homes. They still provide faithful examples of life and witness, still exercise their God-given gifts and abilities. And Proverbs still encourages us to recognize women's worth and work.

As we do so, we need not limit ourselves to certain letters of the alphabet or to a patriarchal point of view. Instead, we need to claim the whole experience of women, including women's friendships and women's participation in intellectual, political, economic, and religious life. Then women may truly receive a fair share of their labor and a rightful place in the city gates.

Meditation Focus: In what ways have you received public recognition for your work both inside and outside of the home? In what ways have you missed the credit due you?

Prayer: We have been taught to be modest and self-effacing, to work unselfishly and without thought of gain, and we do not want to discard what is good in that teaching. But at the same time, we need to know that our work is worthwhile to God and to others. May God grant us a healthy balance: to be humble and yet honest about our accomplishments, to give and also to receive the support and affirmation of others. Amen.

How Fair and Pleasant

Scripture Reading: Song of Songs 7:1-9

The Bible is full of surprises. Sandwiched between Ecclesiastes' solemn wisdom and Isaiah's prophetic word, the holy Scriptures present us with the playful and highly erotic Song of Songs. The poem is frankly physical, earthy, sensual. It might almost carry a warning: completely concerned with sex. What are we to make of its praise of thighs, navel, belly, breasts? Does such a book really belong in the Bible?

Commentators throughout history have tried to solve these questions by interpreting the Song of Songs in terms of the relationship between God and an individual worshiper. The beloved's search for her lover is like the soul's search for God. The lover's praise of the beloved is like Christ's love for the church. From the ancient Jews to the scholars of the Reformation, various commentators have worked with such an interpretative framework.

Unfortunately, this view of the Song resulted in so many different interpretations that the meaning of the Song still remained unclear. In addition, the Song itself gives no indication that it should be interpreted in terms of God and the human soul or in terms of Christ and the church. Why not simply take it at face value and on its own terms?

Some scholars have tried to do exactly that. For them, the Song makes more sense as a collection of love poems written by Solomon or some other poet. It may be an anthology of poems loosely based on the seven-day Syrian wedding feast. Or it may be a unified poem-story about a young woman loved both by a king and by a shepherd.

As one of these love poems, our Scripture reading records a lover's rhapsody over the beauty of his beloved. Her feet are graceful, her thighs like jewels, her nose a tower, her hair like purple. While some of these metaphors may seem unflattering in the context of our culture, in the context of the poem these were evidently intended as high praise. The woman is fair and pleasant, delectable, stately.

Although the description is frankly sexual, it is really not as inappropriate to the biblical text as it might first appear. The words simply provide a more detailed and more vivid description of the creation which God pronounces good in Genesis. The Song of Songs takes that pronouncement one step further by celebrating the physical beauty of woman and man (e.g., 1:9-17; 4:1-15; 5:10-16; 6:4-10) and the garden that they share (2:8-17; 6:2-3).

In addition, it is important to note that the sexuality of the Song takes place in the context of a continuing love relationship. While there is no mention of marriage in the text itself, the story has most often been interpreted as married love, even as a wedding feast. Certainly there is evidence of a strong, continuing relationship between lover and beloved: "love is strong as death" and "many waters cannot quench love" (8:6b, 7a).

Today the Song of Songs can help us develop a whole and healthy attitude toward love and human sexuality. In the Song, love is both sacred and sexual, wholehearted and whole-bodied, playful yet committed. Sex is both personally satisfying and pleasing to one's partner, an expression of genuine emotion and a delight for the senses.

This biblical vision provides an alternative to the distortions of love and sexuality which abound in our own day. In the world, love is too often reduced to a temporary feeling of emotion, and sex is too often trivialized as an advertising ploy or a one-night stand. At the opposite extreme, some religious circles view sex as sacred, but not fun; for procreation, but not for celebration.

In contrast, the Song of Songs sets love and sex in the context of commitment and claims them both as part of God's good creation. God made us body and soul and calls us good. Man cleaves to woman with joy and enduring commitment, and they become one flesh (6:3a; Gen. 2:23-25).

Meditation Focus: How do you feel about your own body? Can you celebrate it as a great work and gift of God?

Prayer: Creator God, thank you for making us creatures of both body and spirit. We take delight in your gifts of sight and hearing, smell and taste and touch. Help us to use them in responsible and healthy ways for your glory. In the name of Jesus, who took on human flesh for our sake. Amen.

My Beloved and My Friend

Scripture Reading: Song of Songs 7:10-8:4

Our second reading from the Song of Songs is again rich with sexual imagery, as the beloved replies to her lover's praise. She gladly accepts his compliments and invites him out to the garden, used here and elsewhere as a symbol of love-making (e.g., 4:10-16; 5:1). She mentions the many plants of the garden, including the mandrake, which was associated with sexual arousal (Gen. 30:14-16). She speaks frankly of her lover's desire for her and of her own longing for her lover's embrace. Like the rest of the Song, this passage is unashamedly sensual.

As mentioned earlier, however, the Song presents this male and female sexuality in the context of a committed love relationship. Here we might go further and say that the relationship of the two lovers is also one of equality and mutuality. In this passage, the woman takes the initiative in love-making; in another place, it is her lover who suggests it (2:10-15). Both woman and man take delight in and praise one another's bodies (e.g., 4:1-15; 5:10-16). Both seek one another and call out to one another (3:1-5; 5:2-8). Both apparently work as shepherds (1:7-8; 2:16). In life and in love, woman and man are partners.

With this picture of mutuality, the Song provides a model for those of us today who are writing our own song of songs with our own beloved partners. We are invited to the same commitment of love, the same partnership of give and take. Like this unnamed couple, we need not follow conventional male-female roles if they do not fit us. Neither do we need to adopt unconventional roles for their own sake. Instead, we are invited to be honest with one another, to be ourselves with one another, as God created us to be.

For some of us, this interpretation and application of the Song of Songs may be encouraging as a biblical alternative to the distorted relationships we see in our world today. With the Song, we want to affirm marriage as an intimate partnership, not simply a legal contract or a social institution. We welcome the Song's vision of marriage as a relationship of equals bound together by love, not as a hierarchy or a standard set of roles to play. We are challenged by this picture of woman and man as partners in God's good garden.

And yet for others of us, this version of the Song of Songs may seem too idealistic, too unrealistic, too far removed from the lives that we really live. What does the Song have to say to single people? What does it have to say to those who do not have this kind of love relationship with their spouses?

Perhaps some of the same principles may be applied to our relationships with one another even outside of marriage. In our not-so-intimate relationships, we may still respect one another as equals, still appreciate one another as gifts from God, still work together as friends and colleagues. These ways of relating, which are so fundamental to a good marriage, are basic to all other human relationships as well.

At this point, we might also employ a somewhat more symbolic interpretation of the Song. After all, whether or not the Song was intended as an allegory of God's love for humankind, the truth is that all human love reflects the divine love at least to some degree. The love between parent and child, between husband and wife, between friends gives us a glimpse of God's love for humankind. Likewise in the Song of Songs, beloved and lover show us something of God's love and longing for us.

And so in all our relationships—as wives and husbands, as friends and colleagues, as worshipers and lovers of God—may we be able to say: "This is my beloved and this is my friend" (5:16).

Meditation Focus: How much can you identify with the two lovers portrayed in this Song? At what points do you have difficulty identifying with them?

Prayer: O God, your word makes us appreciate again our capacity for love and intimacy. Thank you for family and friends, for our intimate relationships and our more casual acquaintances. As we cherish these human ties, remind us also that even the most intimate and most satisfying human love can never match the relationship that we may have with you. Amen.

Ones With Authority

Scripture Reading: Isaiah 3:13-4:1

Since Isaiah's unnamed daughters of Zion first appear only in verse 16, one might well ask why our Scripture reading begins several verses earlier. Why include Isaiah's words addressed to the men of Israel? Why include a few verses about how they treated the poor when the rest of the passage apparently addresses women about their personal pride and extravagance?

Once again, we must not judge our text too quickly. On closer inspection, it becomes clear that Isaiah's charge against the women of Jerusalem is not really one of personal vanity. In fact, the prophet's complaint against the men and women of Jerusalem is really the same: as leaders of the people, both had abused their authority.

Instead of exercising their leadership in obedience to God and for the good of others, these men and women had used their authority to become rich at the expense of the poor (v. 14), to oppress the people they were supposed to lead (v. 15), to be proud (v. 16a), and to call attention to themselves (v. 16b).

That the prophet addresses himself to the leaders of the people is apparent in the items he lists in the heart of the passage (vv. 18-23). Most of these are not used by ordinary folk in the Bible, but appear only in connection with figures of leadership, like kings, queens, and members of the priesthood. The signet ring is most clearly associated with royalty as in the book of Esther (Esther 3:10, 12; 8:2, 8, 10). Less obvious are the crescents worn by the kings of Midian (Judg. 8:26) and the turban worn by the high priest Joshua (Zech. 3:5).

The items in Isaiah's list also indicate that the prophet does not address himself only to women, for many of the items listed are used elsewhere in the Bible only by men. For example, Samson offers linen garments to his male guests as the reward for answering his riddle (Judg. 14:12, 13), and King Ahasuerus gives his signet ring to Mordecai (Esther 8:2). Even the handbags are used by the Syrian army commander Naaman, although the word there is simply translated "bags" (2 Kings 5:23).

In these and other places in the Bible, such outward symbols of authority are not condemned, but instead regarded as appropriate symbols of honor.

Only here in Isaiah, because the leaders had abused their authority, does the prophet speak out against these things. The real issue is not the use of perfume, but the abuse of authority; not beautiful clothes, but shameful behavior.

Because of their corrupt leadership, both men and women would lose the outward symbols of honor and the leadership and authority that such symbols represented. Both would lose their fine fragrances. Both would be taken prisoner. Both would wear sackcloth instead of rich garments. Both would know shame instead of beauty. Jerusalem itself would be emptied of its people, and war would mean such a loss of life that there would be seven women for every remaining man.

While Isaiah addresses this stinging rebuke to a specific people at a specific point in history, his emphasis on right leadership may still speak to us in our own day. God still desires faithful leaders who will exercise authority with care.

Unlike Isaiah's unnamed daughters of Zion, we may not be leading public figures in our own nations. But all of us have certain leadership responsibilities and areas of personal authority. As citizens of our own countries, we speak to our governments. As church elders or Sunday school teachers, we are leaders and role models in our churches. At home, we parent our children and exercise authority over our household budgets. At work, we may supervise other workers or wield authority in certain areas of expertise. In each of these areas, God calls us to be faithful leaders.

Meditation Focus: Think of one area of leadership or authority in your own life. How can you use it in obedience to God and for the good of others?

Prayer: O God, where we have failed to be the leaders you have called us to be, where we have used our authority for our own ends, we ask for your forgiveness and a new resolve to be faithful leaders. May we learn to follow Jesus as our perfect leader, who used his authority over nature to calm storms and to heal disease, who used his authority over people to call them to love God and one another. Amen.

Queens of Earth

Scripture Reading: Jeremiah 44:15-19

Once again, we pick up the biblical story in the middle of the action. The place is Pathros, Egypt, the date some time after the Babylonians had captured and destroyed Jerusalem. The occasion is a public meeting between the prophet Jeremiah and a group of Israelite people living in exile.

Just before the verses of our reading, Jeremiah had pronounced God's judgment against these unnamed women and men for their idolatry. According to the prophet, the people had made offerings to other gods and were thus in danger of cutting themselves off from the one true God (44:8). They were committing the same sin that had resulted in the destruction of Jerusalem (44:2, 3; cf. 7:17, 18).

Now in our Scripture passage, the people reply to Jeremiah. Far from denying his charge of idolatry, the people freely admit and boldly defend the sacrifices they have made. They disagree with Jeremiah's interpretation of events. They claim that their troubles had begun only once they had ceased worshipping the queen of heaven. In their opinion if they had not stopped, they might still be in Jerusalem and Judah.

And so the people declare their intention to continue their idolatry. They will keep the vows they have made to the goddess. They will pour out their libations and make cakes that bear her image. Stubbornly, they refuse to heed the prophet's warning to return to the God of Israel.

Neither Jeremiah nor the people address the false goddess by name. To these Israelites who had adopted her worship, she was simply the queen of heaven. To the Assyrians, she was Ishtar. To the Canaanites, she was Ashtoreth. To all of them, she was the goddess of life, the one who ensured safe childbirth and healthy children, the one who offered protection from disease and death.

More specifically for these Israelites in Egypt, the queen of heaven had become the goddess of peace and prosperity. In the past when they had worshipped her, the Babylonians had left them alone. Their crops had flourished. They had lacked nothing—or at least that was the way it had seemed to them. It only made sense to secure their future good fortune by worshipping the queen of heaven.

It is not difficult to understand the attraction of such a religious cult. Even today women and men alike still long for peace and prosperity, for health and security, for the promise of life. And even today there are various idols—what we might call queens of earth—that appear to offer us these things.

At times, money may appear to be the queen of earth. It teases us with a false sense of security: If we only had money, we would never go hungry or lack anything. We would not have to fear old age or ill health. And so we make sacrifices on behalf of money. We pour out our time and energy like a drink offering. We allow the desire for money to shape our work, our play, and even our friendships, like so many cakes stamped with the image of a false goddess.

At other times, military strength may appear to be the queen of earth. Again, it tempts us with a false sense of security: If only we had a strong army to deter our enemies, then we would have peace. We could protect our food and oil supply and never lack anything. And so we make sacrifices for the sake of the military. We sacrifice food, health, and other social programs, so we can build weapons enough to destroy the earth many times over. We pour out the lives of men and women like a drink offering. We allow the military and military solutions to stamp their image on our national and international relationships.

Money, military, health, education, full employment, family. In their proper place, these may be gifts from God. But as objects of worship, they are only idols, queens of earth to tempt us away from true faith and true worship. The challenge of Jeremiah to the unnamed women of Pathros is a challenge to us still: Leave the idols of earth, and worship God alone.

Meditation Focus: What other possible "queens of earth" can you identify besides the ones mentioned above? How do you handle the temptation they present?

Prayer: Great Giver of life, keep us from all false gods. When we are tempted to put our trust in money, may we remember that our true security is in you. When we are tempted to put our trust in the military, may we remember that our true defense is your strength. In the name of Jesus, our Savior and Sovereign. Amen.

Room at the Table

Scripture Reading: Matthew 15:21-28

As just one story in a whole string of healing stories, Jesus' encounter with the Canaanite woman might seem rather unremarkable at first. By that time, Jesus had already healed a man with leprosy, a centurion's servant, Peter's mother-in-law, a paralyzed man, two blind men, and a multitude of others with various afflictions.

But the writer of Matthew begins this account with a detail that would have been sure to catch the readers' interest: the woman was a Canaanite. To us, this might seem insignificant, but to the gospel's first readers, it made all the difference in the world. In their time, Jews and Canaanites simply did not have anything to do with one another. They belonged to different cultures, different religions, different histories. Their mutual hostility was centuries old and still strong. A Canaanite coming to Jesus for help would be as shocking as a Hatfield seeking advice from a McCoy, or a capitalist approaching a communist during the Cold War.

The woman must have been desperate even to think of approaching Jesus. She had to step out of her own background and her own religion to come to him. She risked criticism from her family and her neighbors for reaching out to a Jew. But she came to Jesus and his disciples anyway—not even secretly, but in the open street.

At first Jesus ignored her cries, and his disciples urged him to send her away. To us, their response seems surprisingly unsympathetic, but to the woman, it was probably quite predictable. What more could a Canaanite expect from a group of Jews?

But the woman persisted, until finally Jesus spoke directly to her. "It is not fair to take the children's food and throw it to the dogs," he said (v. 26). Again to us, Jesus seems uncharacteristically harsh; to the Canaanite woman, however, his words likely came as no surprise.

In fact, the woman seemed to take Jesus' comment as an invitation for further dialogue. At last Jesus had spoken to her and given her an opening. She agreed with him, and then boldly used his saying to make her own point: "Yes, Lord, yet even the dogs eat the crumbs that fall from their masters' table" (v. 27).

This time it was Jesus' turn to agree. He admired the woman's determination and her sense of humor as she claimed a place for herself in God's household. She had overcome her own prejudice against the Jews. She had braved the disapproval of her own family and people. She had ignored the disciples' embarrassment over her presence. She had persisted in spite of Jesus' silence and in spite of his apparent refusal of help. She had turned these obstacles into opportunities and counted herself a part of God's community.

The Canaanite woman offers us a positive example for our own lives today. Do we need God's healing touch? Then let us follow the example of the Canaanite woman, and come to Jesus. Does the church seem embarrassed by our presence? Does it exclude us because of our racial background, our culture, our sex, or other differences? Then let us remember the woman of Canaan, and believe that God accepts us just as we are. Is God silent? Does God seem to answer us only with a riddle or with an apparently unreasonable rebuke? Then let us continue to speak to God, and wait for a definite answer.

When we face various obstacles to our faith, or when we feel excluded in some way from the community of faith, it is easy to become discouraged, to lose our sense of humor, to become bitter, and to turn away from God and the church. But the Canaanite woman's encounter with Jesus teaches us a better way of dealing with such difficulties: Continue to come, continue to dialogue. God's silence will not last forever; even God's apparent rebuke may not be the final word. There is room for us all at God's table.

Meditation Focus: Have you ever felt shut away from God or from the church? How did you respond to your situation? In what ways have you excluded others from God's household?

Prayer: O God, we confess that we do not always understand your silence. We do not always understand your answers. Yet we ask for persistence in prayer, for patience to wait for your word to us, and for discernment to understand your meaning. In the name of Jesus, who invites us all to come to you. Amen.

Eat and Be Satisfied

Scripture Reading: Matthew 15:29-39

Each of the four gospels tells at least one story about Jesus feeding a large crowd of people. But only the gospels of Matthew and Mark say that Jesus does this twice during his public ministry, and only the first gospel departs from the custom of numbering only the men in the crowd. At both the feeding of the 5000 men and at the feeding of the 4000 men, Matthew adds the detail "besides women and children" (v. 38, cf. 14:21). Without the gospel of Matthew, we would never have known the women were even there.

Like the men in the second crowd of over 4000 people, these women probably came from the many small villages along the Sea of Galilee. These were busy women, women who might otherwise have been drawing water or grinding grain or baking bread or sweeping floors or spinning yarn or selling goods or making clothes for the poor or doing any number of other useful tasks and good works.

Instead, they left their homes and marketplaces and all their chores to be with Jesus. They came with their husbands and their children. They came with their own need for healing and brought with them others who needed healing too. For three days, they listened to Jesus' teaching, they received his healing, and they offered praise to God.

Then, tired and hungry, they prepared to return home. But Jesus was not quite ready to dismiss them. As he had done before at an earlier gathering, he told the people to sit down. Once again, he took bread and fish, blessed them and broke them and gave them to his disciples to serve to the crowd. And once again, there was more than enough food for everyone. All could eat and be satisfied.

Today, we too are busy women, women who might be cooking a meal or preparing a Sunday school lesson or volunteering at the prison or studying for an exam or running a business or organizing a community group or doing any number of other good works. But as these unnamed women left their daily responsibilities for a time to be with Jesus, so we too may be free to leave our responsibilities for a time.

This is not to minimize the real hunger that exists in the world, the real needs that God has called us to meet. Like Jesus, we too need to have compassion on hungry people, to feed them lest they perish. Like the disciples in this story, we too need to be faithful servants, carrying out the responsibilities that God has given us.

But sometimes we also need to be like the unnamed women, men, and children of this story, who left their daily responsibilities to sit at Jesus' feet. God invites us to come away for a time from our homes and marketplaces and all our good works to be with Jesus, to come for teaching, healing, worship, and nourishment.

Such nourishment comes to us in many different ways. Some of us may receive it most fully during our time spent in community: God meets us in Sunday morning worship, nourishes us in the celebration of the Lord's Supper, laughs with us as we share a meal with friends. For others, such renewal comes most fully during time spent alone: God speaks to us in the silence of a weekend retreat, teaches us in our daily Bible reading and prayer, heals us as we spend time in meditation, journaling, and silence. For still others, nourishment comes through more physical activities: God touches us as we listen to music, refreshes us as we work in our gardens, lifts our spirits as we take a long walk before supper.

In these and many other ways, God longs to nourish us so that we too might not faint on our way through life. The invitation is open. Come, rest for a while. Eat, and be satisfied.

Meditation Focus: Re-read the paragraph that talks about the different ways God nourishes us. Which do you find nourishing? Which are draining? What other nourishing activities would you add to the list for yourself?

Prayer: *O God, who had compassion on the crowds, have compassion also on us. Draw us near to listen to your voice, to experience healing, to offer our praise, to be nourished by you. As you multiplied the loaves and fishes by the Sea of Galilee, so multiply our faith and hope and love that we might not faint, but go forward renewed for life and service in your name. Amen.*

A Place of Honor

Scripture Reading: Matthew 20:20-28

The mother of the sons of Zebedee is mentioned only twice in the gospel of Matthew: here, to request a favor of Jesus, and later, to witness Jesus' crucifixion (27:56). Both times she appears only briefly, and both times she is identified only as the unnamed mother of unnamed sons.

Most of what we know of this woman must be pieced together from other passages of the Bible. She was a Jew and probably a native of Galilee (4:18). Her husband, Zebedee, was a fisherman (4:21). Her two sons were James and John, both former fishermen and both disciples of Jesus (4:21, 22). Her name was likely Salome (27:56; cf. Mark 15:40), and she was probably a sister to Mary, the mother of Jesus (27:56; cf. John 19:25).

In addition to these specific biographical details, we might further identify this woman as a disciple of Jesus. When she appears in the gospel of Matthew, she appears both times in the company of Jesus' other disciples. She evidently travelled with Jesus, for she was with him in Jericho where she asked him for a favor and with him again outside of Jerusalem where she witnessed his crucifixion. She was one of the faithful who had listened to his teaching, wondered at his miracles, and followed him even to the cross.

But just after Jesus' third prediction of his coming death, this unnamed disciple came to Jesus with a surprising request. For herself, she asked nothing; but for her two sons, she asked for two seats of honor in Jesus' kingdom.

As a disciple of Jesus, the mother of James and John should have known better than to make such a request. She had heard Jesus' teaching about his coming suffering and death. She had seen Jesus' own life of humility and service. Why then would she ask Jesus to give her sons places of honor in his kingdom?

From the details of the story, it is clear that the woman did so at the request of her two sons. Certainly Jesus himself understood that to be the case, for he did not reply directly to her, but to James and John. The other disciples also assumed that the two brothers were the real source of the request; when the disciples heard about it, they directed their anger not at the mother, but at her sons. Furthermore, in the gospel of Mark's account of the same incident, the mother of James and John is not even mentioned (Mark 10:35-45). Clearly the woman did not initiate the request herself, but spoke to Jesus at the urging of her two sons.

Yet even as a spokesperson for the two men, the mother of James and John was not entirely blameless. In her willingness to ask Jesus to honor her sons, she was guilty of trying to please others instead of following what she knew to be Jesus' teaching of servanthood. In making her request on their behalf, perhaps she was also guilty of trying to live her life through her sons and their accomplishments instead of taking responsibility for her own life.

Of course it is only natural to want the best for our children. Even Jesus did not rebuke the mother of James and John for her misguided request. But our children do not always ask for the best things. And so instead of simply giving in and going along with their desires, we need to give them God's best: to let them see our own commitment to Jesus and so encourage them to follow him.

At the same time, we need to avoid the temptation of living our lives through our children, of trying to make their successes our own. Just as we cannot fulfill their every desire, neither can they be happy or successful or committed to Jesus on our behalf. All of us need to be responsible for our own walk with God.

In the end, the mother of James and John did demonstrate that personal responsibility. While her sons deserted Jesus, she followed her Lord right to the cross. And as she stood there, it was she—and not her sons—who occupied a place of honor next to Jesus.

Meditation Focus: In what ways have you been tempted to please others instead of pleasing God? How have you been tempted to live through others instead of taking responsibility for your own life?

Prayer: We have the honor of following Jesus. God grant us the faith and endurance to follow to the end. Amen.

The Day and the Hour

Scripture Reading: Matthew 25:1-13

Throughout the history of biblical interpretation, this simple story has generated a host of not-so-simple questions. Is the story an allegory or a parable? Does the oil represent faith or the Holy Spirit, or is it just a detail of the story? Were the wise young women also selfish because they would not share their oil? Why does the bridegroom recognize the women on the street but not the ones on his doorstep? Would ten unsupervised young women be on their way to a wedding late at night? Would the sellers have been open for business at midnight? Does this story accurately reflect first-century Jewish culture, or is it completely fanciful?

Such questions are both interesting and legitimate, but they are also somewhat removed from the text itself. They take us beyond the story and its context into the areas of literary classification, psychology, culture, and history. Our question, however, is much more focused: What does the story say to us when taken on its own terms?

The story begins with ten young women waiting for the start of a wedding feast. All ten become drowsy during the long wait, and all ten fall asleep. When a shout finally announces the bridegroom's arrival, the ten women wake up. Five of them have just enough extra oil to relight their lamps; but the other five have no oil left at all, and they hurry to the sellers to buy some. When the five women return with their oil, they discover that everyone has already gone in to the wedding feast. Hoping to gain a late entrance, they knock on the door, but the bridegroom refuses to let them in. Here the story ends, and Jesus then provides his own interpretive key: "Keep awake therefore, for you know neither the day nor the hour" (v. 13).

Perhaps if the women had stayed awake, they would have seen their lamps burning low and would have noticed their lack of oil earlier. Other than that, there seems to be no reason for Jesus to focus on the idea of staying awake. After all, in the story even the wise young women fall asleep and yet go unrebuked.

So the five foolish women are not left out of the wedding feast because they fall asleep, for all ten women fall asleep. The five are not left out because they have no oil, for they return with oil from the sellers. No, the women are left out of the wedding feast because they are unprepared at the appointed time. This idea of timing is underscored by the second part of Jesus' warning: "for you know neither the day nor the hour."

The women really needed to be ready whenever the bridegroom arrived. But they were caught at an unprepared moment and so missed the opportunity to join the celebration. By the time they were ready, the opportunity had passed. They were too late. They had arrived at the right place, but at the wrong time.

The story of these foolish young women has most often been interpreted in terms of Christ's final return: Our Savior will return in person one day, and we need to be ready when that unknown day and hour arrives. Such an interpretation fits the story and its context in the larger discourse about Christ's return and God's final judgment (24:36-25:46).

But this story may also apply to our lives in a more general sense, for Christ comes to us not just at the end of time, but in many different ways every day. We may meet Jesus in a quiet time of prayer or feel his presence at a noisy family meal. We may see Jesus' love in the eyes of a friend or hear his laugh in the laughter of a child. Jesus may work beside us in the office or ask us for spare change on the street.

Each day Christ comes to us as suddenly and as unexpectedly as he will come at the end of time. Now is the appointed time. Let us be ready to welcome him today and tomorrow whenever he comes to us.

Meditation Focus: How have you experienced Jesus' coming in your own life this past week?

Prayer: O God, give us ears to hear your call in our lives, and make us ready to respond. We want to be ready to welcome Jesus every day and every hour. In the name of our Savior, for whom we wait in expectation. Amen.

Serving Like Jesus

Scripture Reading: Mark 1:29-34

In its usual clipped style, the gospel of Mark gives us just the bare bones of a story. One sabbath day after Jesus had finished teaching in the synagogue, Jesus and some of his disciples went to Simon and Andrew's house. When they arrived, they found Simon's mother-in-law sick with fever. Jesus went to her bedside, laid his hand on hers, raised her up, and healed her of her illness. Then Simon's mother-in-law "began to serve" Jesus and the others (v. 31).

Even in this brief account, the gospel writer takes care to record the response of Simon's mother-in-law: she got up from her bed and began to serve. Her body immediately responded to Jesus' healing power, and her spirit immediately responded to the need for service. Her family and guests had just arrived from the synagogue and needed water and oil to wash and refresh themselves, food and drink to share a meal together.

Yet the gospel suggests that the woman's service went deeper than this traditional Jewish hospitality. The Greek word used to describe her service in this passage is the very same word that Jesus uses to describe his own service in Mark 10:45: "For the Son of Man came not to be served but to serve, and to give his life a ransom for many." The same word used in the two places links together the service rendered by Simon's mother-in-law and the service performed by Jesus. That link between the two raises an important question: In what ways was the woman's service Christ-like?

First of all, for both Simon's mother-in-law and for Jesus, serving was a priority. On that sabbath day, Jesus had cleansed a man of an unclean spirit and healed Simon's mother-in-law. On other sabbaths he would cure a man with a withered hand (Mark 3:1-6), heal a crippled woman (Luke 13:10-17), and make a blind man see (John 9:1-34). For Jesus, serving was more important than a slavish observance of religious tradition.

When Jesus healed Simon's mother-in-law on the sabbath, he set her free to make serving a priority in her own life. She served Jesus that sabbath day, even though her work might have technically broken the law of sabbath rest. She served Jesus, even though such contact between men and women was not permitted by some of the rabbis. Simon's mother-in-law followed Jesus' example by making service more important than blind obedience to religious law.

Second, Jesus served out of a sense of his own identity and his own wholeness. He was the Son of Man and the Lord of the sabbath (Mark 2:28), who knew he had come from God and was going to God (John 13:3). He did not serve out of guilt or a need for approval from others. His service sprang from his own wholeness and resulted in wholeness for others.

When Jesus healed Simon's mother-in-law, he set her free to serve out of a sense of her own wholeness. She did not serve simply because it was traditional for her to do so. She served because Jesus had made her whole.

As the first healing in the gospel of Mark, the healing of Simon's mother-in-law was just a foretaste of all the healings that would follow. That evening after the sabbath had ended, Jesus healed many more people of their illnesses and cast out many evil spirits. Throughout his earthly ministry, he continued to cure leprosy, banish paralysis, restore hearing and sight, and exorcise demons.

Jesus continues to heal today. Like Simon's mother-in-law, we too can be touched by Jesus and receive fresh motivation for service. We no longer need to serve out of a sense of guilt or a need for approval or traditional role playing. Instead, we can make service a priority and serve out of a sense of our wholeness in Jesus Christ.

Meditation Focus: Think of a specific area of your own service to God and others. What motivates you for service?

Prayer: O God, we confess that we have not always made service a priority in our lives. When we have tried to serve you, we have not always served out of wholeness and joy, but out of guilt and our own need. Touch our lives as you touched the life of Simon's mother-in-law. Make us whole and give us fresh vision and motivation for service. Amen.

The First Lazarus

Scripture Reading: Mark 5:21-24a, 35-43

During his earthly ministry, Jesus raised three people from the dead: Jairus' daughter, the son of an unnamed widow, and Lazarus. Of these three people, Lazarus is probably the most well known and widely studied, but Jairus' daughter was actually the first person in the gospel records to be brought back to life by Jesus. She was the first Lazarus.

As in the later story of Lazarus, the story of Jairus' daughter began with a request to Jesus for healing. And, in a similar fashion, there was a delay, a death, Jesus' apparently too late arrival, his call to have faith, and finally a miraculous restoration of life.

Jesus' command to Jairus' daughter yielded immediate results. In spite of the skepticism of the waiting crowd of mourners, the girl rose from the dead. Her healing was not a partial one nor one that required a long period of recuperation. It was both immediate and complete.

At Jesus' touch and by his word, the girl returned to normal life. She opened her eyes and rose from her bed. She walked around the room. She took food and drink from her parents. Once the crowd of mourners had laughed at Jesus; now it was the girl's turn to laugh with joy over her recovered strength. Now she could resume her place in her family and among her friends. She could look forward to growing up and becoming an adult.

This was the first time that Jesus had called someone back to life, but he did not want the miracle made public. Instead, he charged those who witnessed it to keep the matter confidential. He took care to guard the girl's privacy and to allow her to return to normal life.

This is a key point of the story: When Jesus healed Jairus' daughter, he returned her to ordinary life. He did not make her into some kind of sideshow freak as the first person he raised from the dead. He did not use her to publicize his ministry. He simply allowed her to become again an ordinary girl on the brink of womanhood, able to rise and walk, to speak, to laugh, to run, to eat, to drink. These very ordinary activities were enough to proclaim the miraculous work of God. They were enough to cause all those present to be filled with wonder.

This story is special because of this celebration of normal life. It celebrates the ability to get out of bed as if from a good night's sleep. It celebrates the gift of physical strength, of standing and walking, of laughing and praising, of eating and drinking. It reminds us that everyday life is precious and made for joy and praise.

As children, we once knew this great delight in daily life. We liked long, meandering walks that went no place in particular. We liked the crunch of carrots and the way ice cream felt on our tongues. We liked games and good jokes and playing with our friends. At night we went to bed only reluctantly no matter how tired we were, for we did not want to miss a single exciting minute of our day.

But somehow as we grew up into teenagers and adults, we also outgrew that wonder. Now it seems as if we walk as little as possible. We eat without tasting, often too quickly, often choosing fast food that is neither nourishing nor fun nor pleasing to the palate. We wake up tired and reluctant to face another day of work and miss the sheer wonder of life itself.

But even for grownups, daily life does not need to be so flat and uninteresting. Instead, like Jairus' daughter, we too can recover the wonder of life. The same God who brought her from death to life can raise us up from dreariness to joy. The same Jesus who touched her life can also touch ours. The same Spirit who opened her eyes can also give us a new vision for life's meaning. God created life, and it was—and is—good. Thanks be to God.

Meditation Focus: What areas of ordinary life do you tend to take for granted? How might you recapture a sense of wonder and thanksgiving to God?

Prayer: Creator God, we thank you for the gift of life. Open our eyes again to the wonder of your creation and to our place in it. Touch our lives with the miraculous, so that we might be overcome with joy and praise to you. Amen.

Call Me Daughter

Scripture Reading: Mark 5:24b-34

Jesus might have kept on walking. The crowd pressed around him and moved him forward. Jairus was at his side, urging him on toward the house where Jairus' daughter lay close to death. Even when Jesus felt the healing power go out of him, he really had no need to stop. After all, whoever had touched him had already been healed, and there was more urgent work ahead.

So then why did Jesus stop? Did it really matter who had touched him? Why not let the woman go her own way healed by her touch and undetected by the crowd? Why not continue uninterrupted on his own way toward Jairus' house?

Jesus' insistence on stopping at this point becomes clearer when we learn a little more about the woman. Our text says that she had been afflicted with hemorrhages for twelve years. According to Jewish law, that meant that she had been ceremonially unclean for twelve years (Lev. 15:25ff.). She could not touch anyone else without making that person unclean as well. She could not take part in normal Jewish religious and social life.

And so this woman suffered under a double burden of chronic illness and chronic uncleanness. Her chronic illness and long, unsuccessful search for a cure had left her physically exhausted, financially impoverished, and emotionally discouraged. Her chronic uncleanness had kept her physically isolated from other people and spiritually separated from God.

Because of this double burden, the physical healing the woman received when she touched Jesus was not enough. To be completely well, she needed not only an end to her bleeding, but a new beginning of emotional, social, and spiritual wholeness. And perhaps that is why Jesus stopped. He did not want to leave her with only a physical and partial healing; he wanted to make her completely well.

To that end, the first thing that Jesus did was to call the woman out of the crowd of people around him. For the twelve years of her illness and uncleanness, people had avoided the woman. Now Jesus himself interrupted an important errand to meet with her and to listen to her. He listened to the whole truth

71

of her life the way no other physician had ever listened to her before. Her isolation was over at last.

Then after Jesus had heard the woman's story, he pronounced her well. That in itself was nothing new, for she had already felt the healing in her own body. But after twelve years of social and religious isolation, the woman needed to hear that she was truly a daughter in the family of God. After twelve years under the curse of illness and uncleanness, she really needed to hear Jesus' blessing to go in peace. Now she could begin her life again.

Even though Jairus had approached him first, Jesus first chose to identify the woman who had touched him. Even though Jairus was a respected leader of the synagogue, Jesus first listened with respect to an ordinary and, until recently, unclean member of the crowd. Even though Jairus' daughter was about to die, Jesus first reached out to a woman who had already been healed. In his insistence on meeting the woman, Jesus demonstrated that her healing was just as important as the healing of Jairus' daughter.

In sickness or in health, we too need to know that we are accepted and loved as part of God's family. And so, like this woman who approached Jesus, let us also approach God in faith. Let us lay hold of God's compassion. Let us speak the whole truth of our lives. And then let us accept our identity as daughters of God, and go with God's blessing of peace.

Meditation Focus: In what ways have you reached out to God in faith? In what ways has God recognized you, listened to you, and pronounced a blessing on you as a daughter?

Prayer: God, thank you for Jesus' willingness to stop and to care for this unnamed woman. We treasure this story as a wonderful picture of the care that you have for each one of us, for you also heal us and call us daughter. At the same time, we accept this story as an example of the way we should care for others. Today we particularly remember those who suffer from chronic illness. Help us to be sensitive to their needs and to the needs of others. In the name of Jesus, the Great Physician. Amen.

More Than Money

Scripture Reading: Mark 12:41-44

When we think of the story of this poor widow and her two coins, most of us probably think of Christian stewardship. As the widow put all that she had into the temple treasury, so we should give generously to the church—or so we have always been told. But if we read the widow's story in the wider context of the gospel of Mark, we soon discover that it speaks about much more than money.

Before the widow made her entrance into the temple courtyard, Jesus had been speaking to his disciples and the rest of the people about the scribes. He was unmoved by their long robes or their fancy titles. He criticized their pride, their insincerity, and their lack of compassion. He even mentioned their harsh treatment of widows in his critique (12:40).

Then just after the widow's story, as Jesus and his disciples were leaving the temple, one of the disciples stopped to admire the magnificent building and stones of the temple area. But again, Jesus remained unimpressed. He knew the temple was just a building made by human hands, and he predicted its eventual destruction (13:2).

So before the story of the poor widow, we see Jesus unimpressed by the great robes and high rank of the scribes. After her story, we see Jesus unimpressed by the temple with its great architecture. And bracketed by those two things, we have what really impressed Jesus: the widow who put two coins into the temple treasury.

Those two coins were all the poor woman had left to live on, but they would scarcely have been noticed in the temple budget. At that time, a day laborer might have made as much as those two coins in just fifteen minutes of work.

Why did the woman bother with such a small offering? After all, she could have made her prayers at·the temple without making an offering at all. Or she could have put in one coin and kept the other for herself. Yet the poor widow dropped both coins into the temple treasury.

When Jesus saw the widow's offering, he was so impressed that he turned it into a real-life object lesson for his disciples. He called them to his side and said, "Truly I say to you, this poor widow has put in more than all those who are contributing to the treasury" (v. 43b).

The scribes may have acted important. The rich people may have made their large donations. The temple buildings may have looked magnificent. But things were not as they seemed. In Jesus' eyes, the truly great work was the apparently small gift of the poor widow.

As the woman put her two coins into the temple treasury, Jesus saw more than just the money. Not just two small coins. Not just a very small offering in the budget of a very large temple. With her two coins, the widow offered up her whole life to God, and Jesus recognized that total commitment.

As we seek to serve God in our daily lives, sometimes we may feel like poor women, each with a very small offering. The teacher wonders whether she's really making any difference in the lives of her students. The homemaker seems to repeat an endless cycle of cooking and cleaning day after day after day. The church committee member works hard to plan a special missions festival only to find the event poorly attended.

At such times, we may well find ourselves asking, Why bother? Why bother working so hard for so little? What difference does it really make anyway? Yet if God has called us to the work of the home or the church or our community—and surely God has called us—who are we to call it small or insignificant? As Jesus saw more than two coins in the widow's offering, so God sees beyond the physical work of our hands to the commitment we bring to it. What matters is not so much the smallness of what we have to give. What matters is that all of it is committed to God—and then it's as if we have offered our whole lives.

Meditation Focus: What task or activity has God given you that tempts you to ask "Why bother"?

Prayer: Our God, we think now of the various tasks that you have given us at home, in the church, in our neighborhoods and community. Sometimes our part seems so small and insignificant. We get tired of working so hard for so little. We get discouraged by our small results. Help us to re-commit ourselves now to you and to the tasks that you have given us. Amen.

An Unlikely Prophet

Scripture Reading: Mark 14:3-9

The Old Testament prophets were often public figures who spoke both in the courts of kings and in the city streets. We think of men like Moses, who brought God's word to the Pharaoh of Egypt and to his own people. We remember Samuel anointing Saul, and Jeremiah preaching to the crowds at the temple gate.

But in this story of Jesus' anointing, the prophet was neither a man nor a preacher, neither a visitor to the royal court nor a public figure. This New Testament prophet was an unnamed woman, who came to Jesus privately while he sat at table in the house of Simon the leper.

The woman must have seemed out of place in that private room of men. She preached no sermon. She spoke no word at all. Instead, she delivered her prophetic message with an alabaster jar of perfume. In a gesture reminiscent of Old Testament anointings, she held the jar of perfume over Jesus' head and broke the container open. The perfume poured out, and its fragrance filled the room.

The woman's action was prophetic, for it proclaimed Jesus' coming death. Like the bottle of perfume, Jesus' own body would be broken. While the disciples had failed to understand Jesus' teaching about his death, this woman proclaimed the ordeal to come. While others prepared for Jesus' death by plotting to kill him, this woman prepared for his death by anointing him for burial.

The broken jar of perfume was a fitting symbol for Jesus' death. Like the bread Jesus would break at the Last Supper, the broken jar was a reminder of Jesus' broken body. And the perfume released by the jar was a sign that brokenness and death would result in new freedom and new life. Without the broken jar, the scent of perfume would not be released. Without Jesus' death, the resurrection would not happen. Throughout his earthly ministry, Jesus tried to teach his disciples about this paradox of brokenness and wholeness, of death and life. A grain of wheat had to die before it could yield new life. A disciple had to say goodbye to the old way of life before starting the new one. Jesus himself would die and be raised again.

Now at the end of his life, Jesus discovered at least one woman who seemed to understand his teaching. In turn, he understood her prophetic action. Others might criticize her for wasting the perfume, but Jesus commended her. "Let her alone," he said to her critics, "She has anointed my body beforehand for its burial" (vv. 6, 8).

As we read this story of Jesus' anointing, however, we may find ourselves identifying more with the prophet's unnamed critics than with the unnamed prophet herself. Like her critics, we too may quickly dismiss the woman's action as foolish and impractical. Why not rather sell the perfume? Why not give the money to the poor?

Our relationship with the poor is a valid concern, and one that Jesus himself addressed repeatedly during his public ministry. But at this time, Jesus' focus was different—and equally important. His defense of the prophet confirmed her message: Like the alabaster jar, Jesus' body would soon be broken, and new life would be released.

Today as followers of Jesus, we too experience brokenness and wholeness, death and life. And the alabaster jar that expressed that paradox for Jesus expresses it for us as well. Like the alabaster jar, we too will be broken: broken in spirit as we confront sin in our lives, broken in our self-image as we realize our dependence on God, even broken in our beliefs as we grow in the knowledge of the truth.

But as the broken jar released its sweet perfume, so our brokenness may release new life in us as well. Our broken spirits yield a new compassion and humility. Our broken view of self makes way for a new self-identity as a child of God. Our broken beliefs open us to a truer understanding of God and others. Our brokenness can mean positive change and growth.

Meditation Focus: How have you experienced brokenness and death in your own life? Have they also led you to new wholeness and new life? Why or why not?

Prayer: *O God, we thank you for this unlikely prophet and for her message: Brokenness and death are not final, but they can lead us to wholeness and new life. With that promise in mind, we ask you to sustain us in our weakness and to give us new strength to follow and to serve you. In the name of Jesus Christ, whose body was broken for us. Amen.*

Close to Jesus

Scripture Reading: Mark 15:33-41

Although most of Jesus' disciples had left him when he was arrested in the garden of Gethsemane, certain women from his group apparently followed him to the place of crucifixion. Among these witnesses were Mary Magdalene, Mary the mother of James and Joses, Salome, and a number of unnamed women.

Of these unnamed women, the gospel of Mark reports that many had followed Jesus all the way from Galilee to Jerusalem and finally to the cross. They had heard Jesus speak to the crowds in parables. They had watched him heal the blind and free those tormented by demons. They had been at his side when the Jewish authorities criticized him. Now they also stood by to witness his crucifixion.

Yet for all their faithfulness, these women were not quite as close to Jesus as they might have been. They were closer than Jesus' other disciples who had fled at his arrest, but not quite as close as the bystander at the cross who gave Jesus a drink. While they stood near the cross, they did not stand quite as near as the centurion who saw Jesus draw his last breath. According to our text, the women watched only "from a distance" (v. 40).

The women may have been prevented from getting any closer to Jesus by the Roman guards, but they may have also been prevented by their own fear. As devout Jews, they may have been afraid of defiling themselves by coming too near the place of execution. As his close friends and admirers, they may have been afraid to see Jesus' descent into despair and pain. They may even have been afraid of their own possible arrest and execution. And so at his death, even Jesus' closest and most faithful disciples hung back.

At that moment, the women demonstrated a strange mix of faithfulness and not-quite-so-faithfulness. They were faithful enough to follow Jesus to Golgotha, but not quite so faithful to take their place near the cross. They were faithful enough to watch from a distance, but not quite so faithful to stand at Jesus' side. This was the same mixed discipleship that the women would show at the very end of the gospel of Mark. They would be faithful enough to go to Jesus' tomb to anoint his body, but not quite so faithful to respond to the news of Jesus' resurrection without fear. They were disciples of Jesus, but they were not perfect.

As disciples of Jesus, sometimes we too present this same imperfect, mixed discipleship, this same combination of faithfulness and not-quite-so-faithfulness. We may go with Jesus as far as baptism and church membership. We may go as far as regular prayer and tithing our income. But perhaps we still fall short of following Jesus the way we know we should.

We may not want to pray too seriously or too long about our choice of vocation or how we spend our leisure time. We may still want to hold on to some personal grudge. We may be afraid of befriending strangers or working with the poor as Jesus did. We may be reluctant to step beyond our established religious and social traditions. In times and places of religious persecution, we may even be afraid for our own physical safety. In these and other ways, we too may be afraid of getting too close to Jesus.

Fortunately, that is not the end of our story. As disciples of Jesus, we can come to him even with our fears and imperfections. Jesus himself invites us: "Come to me, all you that are weary and are carrying heavy burdens, and I will give you rest. Take my yoke upon you, and learn from me; for I am gentle and humble in heart, and you will find rest for your souls. For my yoke is easy, and my burden is light" (Matt. 11:28-30).

Meditation Focus: How far have you travelled to follow Jesus? How much further do you need to go? What things hold you back from more faithful discipleship?

Prayer: O Faithful God, increase our faithfulness as disciples of Jesus Christ. Where we are fearful, grant us new courage. Where we stumble, forgive us and grant us fresh commitment. Remove the barriers that keep us from you, and draw us close. In the name of Jesus, who suffered and died for our sake and who invites us to come to him. Amen.

Unexpected Grace

Scripture Reading: Luke 7:11-17

In the gospel of Luke, Jesus' parables and healings often appear in pairs: one about a man, the other about a woman. For example in chapter four, Jesus heals a man with an unclean spirit, and then he heals Simon's mother-in-law. In chapter fifteen, he tells a story about a man and his sheep and then a story about a woman and her coin. In chapter eighteen, Jesus tells two parables on prayer: one about the persistent widow and the other about a pious tax collector. Here in chapter seven, he heals a centurion's servant and resurrects a widow's son.

It might seem a bit repetitious and even unnecessary for the gospel to include so many of these doublets. But this multitude of ordinary men and women tells us that Jesus' message is not just for the Pharisees and the scribes and other serious religious people. Instead, Jesus' word addresses each ordinary man and each ordinary woman who hears it.

The widow of Nain was one such ordinary woman. Like other women in her patriarchal culture, she had depended on her husband for her legal status and her livelihood. When he died, she had depended on her only son. But now her son was also dead, and she was more alone than ever. Like other widows who had no sons to care for them, she faced social isolation, poverty, and an uncertain future.

When Jesus saw the woman walking and weeping in the funeral procession, he was filled with compassion. He singled her out for special attention, even though there were many others who mourned the young man. He knew that widows were the poorest of the poor in ancient society. And perhaps he also thought ahead to his own death and to his own mother's coming grief.

No one called out to Jesus from the funeral procession. No one approached him for help. This time, Jesus took the initiative. He moved through the crowd, approached the woman, and offered her words of comfort. "Do not weep," he said (v. 13). The woman looked at him through her tears. Her son had died. How could she not weep?

Jesus came closer still and stepped right up to the open coffin. He touched its wooden frame, looked directly at the young man, and spoke to him. Then to everyone's great amazement and joy, the young man responded by coming back to life. And Jesus restored him to his mother.

Before the raising of Jairus' daughter, Jairus himself had first asked Jesus to heal her. Before the raising of Lazarus, Martha had sent Jesus word of her brother's illness. But in this case, neither the widow nor the crowd had requested Jesus' intervention. God's grace came upon them unexpectedly and independently of their prayers.

Like the widow of Nain, we too are ordinary women. We depend on others, if not for legal status and livelihood as she did, at least for companionship. At times we too experience death in our families and grieve over the loss of loved ones. At times we too feel lonely even when surrounded by a crowd of people.

We know, of course, that God wants us to pray about these life experiences. In the Old Testament, the psalms encourage us to seek God's face (e.g., Pss. 27, 40, 70), and in the New Testament Paul says, "in everything by prayer and supplication with thanksgiving let your requests be made known to God" (Phil. 4:6). Jesus often prayed (Luke 6:12; 22:41-42) and taught his disciples to pray as well (Luke 11:1-4).

But at times when we are too depressed, when words fail us, when we cannot pray, we may still be sure that God sees our tears and hears our unspoken prayers. As Jesus recognized the loss and loneliness of the widow of Nain, so God recognizes our loss and loneliness. As the Holy Spirit moved Jesus to comfort this widow, so the Holy Spirit moves in prayer on our behalf (Rom. 8:26). God takes the initiative and reaches out to us with unexpected grace.

Hear the words of Jesus, the Lord of life: Do not weep. Take heart from the work of Jesus, who raised the widow's son: Resurrection is coming.

Meditation Focus: How have you experienced God's unexpected grace?

Prayer: O God, we thank you for your grace which comes to us in so many unexpected ways. Like the widow of Nain and the crowd that surrounded her, may we learn to respond to it with amazement and praise. Amen.

A Sign of Love

Scripture Reading: Luke 7:36-50

For the second time in the gospel accounts, Jesus is anointed by an unnamed woman. This time the incident occurs not at the end, but in the middle of his public ministry. The place is the house of Simon the Pharisee. The main character is a woman whom the narrator calls a sinner—perhaps a prostitute or simply a woman who did not keep the Jewish religious law.

Whoever this woman was, Simon was shocked to see her in his own home. At a formal banquet such as his, it was not uncommon for uninvited guests to enter the house and stand along the walls to watch the feast. But since this woman was a sinner, she was not only uninvited, but unwelcome, in the house of this strict Pharisee. And to make matters worse, the woman did not stand along the walls with the other uninvited guests, but came near to the guest of honor and touched him.

When the woman first approached Jesus and began to weep and touch his feet, Jesus did not even acknowledge her presence. Instead, he responded to Simon's unspoken criticism with a parable of forgiveness. One debtor had been forgiven little and loved little; the other had been forgiven much and loved much. Even Simon must have understood that Jesus was talking about Simon and the unnamed woman before them.

At the end of the story, Jesus spoke plainly. Simon had felt little need of forgiveness and had shown little love for Jesus: he had given Jesus no water for his feet, no kiss of welcome, no oil for his head. But the woman had been forgiven much and had shown much love: she had washed Jesus' feet with her tears, covered them with kisses, and anointed them with perfume. In her own unique way, the woman had made up for Simon's lack of hospitality.

As a forgiven sinner, the woman showered Jesus with her love. Then as now, it was hardly customary to stand weeping over someone's feet. It was scandalous for a woman to let down her hair in public and highly unconventional to anoint a person's feet with perfume. But instead of criticizing the woman's unorthodox behavior, Jesus accepted it as a sign of her love.

Today women still come forward to minister to Jesus. Like the unnamed woman in our story, we women today are forgiven sinners, prompted to serve out of love for Jesus. Like her, we have unique gifts and unique ways of doing things that can show our love to Jesus and to his church. As her outpouring of love ministered to Jesus, so our service of love may also help to fill existing gaps of ministry.

Like Simon the Pharisee, however, the Simons of today's religious establishment may still respond with disapproval. Some still regard women as uninvited and unwelcome servants within the church, particularly when women serve in leadership roles. For those silent and not-so-silent critics, women's ministry is both untraditional and inappropriate, beyond the bounds of social and religious order. The Simons of our day would rather women stood quietly along the edges of religious life.

But Jesus still graciously accepts and defends the service of women. It may be unorthodox in the eyes of the still predominantly male religious leadership. It may be unexpected and even disturbing to others. It may be imperfect, emotional, even tearful. But when our service arises out of love for Jesus, out of a grateful, forgiven heart, then it is acceptable to God.

So, like the woman who anointed Jesus, let us live as forgiven sinners and show our love to him. Let us not be silenced by our own sense of imperfection or by tradition or by the criticism of others. Instead, let us accept God's forgiveness and respond with all our love and creativity. Let us act in faith and go in peace.

Meditation Focus: What ministry do you offer to Jesus and to the church? What criticism have you faced? How have you dealt with it?

Prayer: Dear Jesus, we have been forgiven much, and so we love much. Help us to serve you out of that love—not because we have anything to prove to others or because we want to put ourselves forward, but because we love you. And once we have our motivation straight, let us serve you honestly and bravely, with sensitivity to your leading and to the needs of others. Amen.

God's Risk-Takers

Scripture Reading: Luke 8:1-3

Throughout the gospels, many women are mentioned by name. Mary, Elizabeth, and Anna appear as major characters in Jesus' birth narrative. Martha and at least two other Marys play significant roles as friends of Jesus. Their names, and the names of others, have their rightful place in Jesus' life and ministry.

But these named women were not the only women who knew and loved Jesus. Around and among them were many other unnamed women as well. In this Scripture passage, for example, Luke mentions Mary, Joanna, and Susanna. But he also marks the presence of other unnamed women with the phrase "and many others" (v. 3). In the Greek text, the word "others" is feminine here, so Luke's phrase might well be translated more clearly "and many other women."

About these other, unnamed, women we know very little. Perhaps Jesus had released some from demons, as he had released Mary Magdalene. Perhaps he had cured some from disease, as he had cured Simon's mother-in-law. Like Joanna, the wife of Herod's steward, some may have been upper-class, married women. Some may also have been wealthy women, as suggested by their financial support of Jesus and the other disciples.

There is simply not enough information to say much more about the backgrounds and identities of these unnamed women. How did they first meet Jesus? Were they really wealthy? Or were they women of limited means who simply gave what little they had? The gospel record is silent. All we know is that these women supported Jesus both financially and by their presence. Like the twelve disciples, these women travelled with Jesus (vv. 1, 2). Like the twelve, they heard his teaching and witnessed his miracles.

These women were risk-takers. They dared to commit their financial resources to Jesus' itinerant ministry. To become disciples of Jesus, they dared to leave their homes, husbands, and children. They defied the social and religious traditions of their day which prevented most women from serious study; they not only studied with their rabbi Jesus, they even dared to travel with him.

Today women are much freer to study, to use their money, to travel, to minister in various capacities. As we seek to follow Jesus, most of us do not face quite the same degree of social and religious disapproval as our foremothers faced. Our family members often follow Jesus with us, as supportive partners on the road of discipleship.

But even for us, risk-taking remains an important part of faith. We need to commit our financial resources to the service of God and others. We need to learn from Jesus and to travel the road of suffering servanthood with him. We need to risk being different and being out of step with our own society.

To follow Jesus in the church means the risk of reaching out to our community, of welcoming people who do not share our ethnic or cultural background. For some of us, it may mean the risk of serving on the church council or spearheading a new service program.

To follow Jesus in our vocations may mean the risk of speaking out against unfair or unsafe working conditions. It may mean leaving familiar surroundings and taking the risk of working overseas. It may mean the risk of going back to school without the assurance of future employment.

Paradoxically, following Jesus might even mean the risk of staying where we are. We may take the risk of working within our own countries, of remaining in the same job or in the same church for many faithful years. We may stay home to raise our children and take the risk of missing a career outside the home. Such specific risks of faith will vary from person to person and from time to time throughout our lives. But if they are truly risks of faith, they will all be part of following Jesus. Like the first women who followed Jesus, we too can step out in faith to learn from him, to witness his work in the world, to join his ministry of sharing the good news of God's dominion. We too can be God's risk-takers.

Meditation Focus: What risks do you need to take to follow Jesus in the church, your vocation, and home life?

Prayer: O God, increase our faith, that we too may become risk-takers with you in ministering to others. In the name of Jesus, who took the risk of becoming human for our sake. Amen.

Yes, But. . . .

Scripture Reading: Luke 11:27-28

One day while Jesus was again teaching a crowd of people, a woman called out to him. This time it was not a cry for help or healing, but a cry of blessing: "Blessed is the womb that bore you and the breasts that nursed you!" (v. 27). It was an unusual and strangely vivid choice of words, meant as a blessing on Jesus' mother, Mary.

This blessing from an unnamed woman of the crowd confirmed Mary's earlier saying in the gospel of Luke. In expectation of Jesus' birth, Mary had said, "Surely, from now on all generations will call me blessed" (1:48b). Now in her own lifetime, her words were already starting to come true as an unnamed woman in the crowd pronounced a blessing.

When Jesus heard those words, he answered them with a blessing of his own: "Blessed rather are those who hear the word of God and obey it!" (v. 28). He did not openly contradict the unnamed woman's blessing, but neither did he let it stand alone unqualified. Instead, he broadened it and changed its emphasis. It was almost as if he were saying, "Yes, but. . . ."

According to Jesus, motherhood alone was no match for hearing and doing the will of God. In fact throughout his ministry, Jesus seemed to discount the importance of motherhood and other family relationships. He called both men and women to a commitment of faith deeper than the commitment of family (9:59-60; 12:51-53). His disciples included both men and women who had left their homes, spouses, and children to be with him (8:1-3). In public, he had even said, "My mother and my brothers are those who hear the word of God and do it" (8:21). For Jesus, the true family was the family of those who heard and obeyed God's word. And the true blessing came not from blood and family ties, but from a right relationship with God.

Even in the case of Mary, Jesus knew that God's blessing did not rest solely on her role as his mother. That was only part of her more primary role as God's servant. Before she was ever Jesus' mother, she was God's handmaiden, a young woman of faith who was prepared to hear and obey the divine word. Mary was part of Jesus' true family not by blood, but by faith. And her true blessing came as a result of her right relationship with God.

And so Jesus could not let the unnamed woman's blessing pass unanswered. That blessing focused too narrowly on just one part of one woman's experience of hearing and obeying the word of God. It missed the larger and more important truth of blessing for all who live faithfully in response to God's word.

Like the unnamed woman in the crowd around Jesus, sometimes we too miss that larger truth. Sometimes we too may overemphasize motherhood and family life as the source of blessing. Sometimes we may focus on the importance of church membership and involvement in ministry. Or we may concentrate on our careers or volunteer activities. We too may have a very limited view of God's blessing.

At such times, Jesus' reply to us is the same reply that he gave the unnamed woman: "Yes, but. . . ." Yes, motherhood and family and church and work life may be gifts from God. Yes, they may be avenues of great blessing—but only as part of our more important role as God's servants. Like Mary, and like the unnamed woman in the crowd, we too are called to hear and obey the word of God.

This is good news for all people. God's blessing is not only for mothers. It is not limited to those related by birth to a certain family or ethnic group. It does not depend on our work in the church or our success in the world. Instead, the divine blessing is open to all of us who hear and obey the word of God.

Meditation Focus: What things do you tend to overemphasize at the expense of hearing and obeying the word of God? How does your attitude to these things change when you consider them in the context of God's will?

Prayer: O God, we confess our narrow-mindedness in limiting your blessing to certain times or places or people or activities. Help us instead to remember that your blessing comes anywhere, any time, and to anyone that hears and obeys your word. Amen.

Transformation

Scripture Reading: Luke 13:10-17

This healing of an unnamed daughter of Abraham is easy to overlook, buried as it is in the middle of a chapter otherwise devoted to Jesus' teaching. Even as the narrator tells the woman's story, it is presented more as an occasion for Jesus' dispute with the ruler of the synagogue than as an important event in the life of a woman. Indeed, the woman and her healing become almost secondary to the debate over the sabbath.

But if we concentrate on the woman herself, we see that her story falls into two very different parts sharply divided by her encounter with Jesus. The two halves together form a more dramatic and profound version of the before and after pictures sometimes found in women's magazines. There a woman might change her appearance, transformed for the moment by a new hair cut, new colors and a change of dress and costume jewelry. Here, this woman undergoes a much more significant transformation from crippled to whole, from stooped over to standing straight. Hers was no temporary or superficial change, but one that was lasting and real.

In this woman's before picture, the gospel writer portrays her almost as a passive object, almost as if her physical weakness had drained her of all other action. She was in the synagogue, she was bent over, but it was Jesus who acted on her behalf. In spite of the ruler's later accusation, the woman did not call any attention to herself at all and did not seek Jesus out for healing. Jesus took the initiative. Only later, in the after picture, does the narrator tell us that the woman became active and praised God.

Before, she must have felt isolated from other people because of her chronic illness. She could not do all of the things that other people could do. Her household chores always took longer than usual. She could not raise her head to look anyone else in the eye. Even going to the synagogue must have been a painful trip for her frail body.

But then Jesus spoke to her and touched her. He broke her isolation and brought her back into the community. When the ruler of the synagogue rebuked her and the other people for seeking healing on the sabbath, Jesus defended her. He recognized her as a daughter of Abraham, and by giving her that title, he affirmed her place in the family of God.

For this woman, meeting Jesus was a major turning point in her life. Before, she was bound by Satan. After, she was freed. Before, she was bent over with disease. After, she could stand straight and was restored to health. Jesus called her, pronounced her restoration to full health, touched her, defended her against her critics, and ended her physical isolation from the community.

For us today, this is a story of hope. We too may suffer some physical ailment that prevents us from living as fully as we might otherwise. We may feel bent out of shape from trying to meet other people's expectations. We may be bowed down with worry or unable to look others in the eye from feelings of insecurity. At times we may feel isolated from our community of neighbors and friends, and even from our own families and church.

Our full restoration may not be all at once like the woman's healing in this story. That may have to wait until we meet our God face to face. And yet this healing of an unnamed woman tells us that God's reign of wholeness has already begun. God is already active on our behalf.

As Jesus met this woman in the synagogue, so God also meets us wherever we are. God speaks to us, pronounces us restored, touches us, defends us against our opponents, and welcomes us as part of the family of God. We need not be isolated, passive, bent over any longer. By God's grace, we too can follow the example of this daughter of Abraham and rise up and praise God.

Meditation Focus: In what ways do you feel bound in your own life? In what ways do you feel free to praise God?

Prayer: O God, we do acknowledge you as the Great Liberator and Healer of all people. Where we are free, may we praise you. Where we are bound, may we place our confidence in you for release. Where we see oppression and brokenness in your world, may we follow you in working for freedom and wholeness. Amen.

Just Like a Woman

Scripture Reading: Luke 15:8-10

How is God like a woman? To some people, this may seem like a blasphemous question, for God is not human and female. To others, such a question may seem simply ridiculous, for God is beyond comparison to any creature. God surpasses all human limitations. God transcends all human categories. Yet in story after story, Jesus himself compared God with ordinary women and men. He showed people how God is like a woman searching for a lost coin or like a man looking for a lost sheep. He taught his disciples that the kingdom of God is like a woman baking bread or like a man sowing seed. Jesus knew how to use the events of daily life to teach people about God.

In his parable of the lost coin, for example, Jesus tried to teach the Pharisees and scribes about God's love for all people. Jesus knew that some of the Jews had been grumbling about his friendships with tax collectors and others who did not keep the Jewish ceremonial law. So to answer their criticisms, he told them three stories: the parable of the lost sheep, the parable of the lost coin, and the parable of the lost son.

All three stories spoke of God's love, but each emphasized a slightly different point. The parable of the lost sheep emphasized God going out into the wilderness. The parable of the lost son focused on God waiting and watching and longing for people to repent. The parable of the lost coin concentrated on God searching for those in need.

Of the three parables, the parable of the lost coin was the only one in which the words "search carefully" occurred (v. 8). The woman lit a lamp, swept the house, and searched carefully. She was very thorough. She went to a great deal of trouble to find her lost coin.

During the time of Jesus, the structure of the typical Palestinian house would have made such a careful search a necessity. Most houses had low ceilings, small doors, and very small windows. Those features made them cooler in the summer and warmer in the winter, but they also made the houses very dark. If the woman was to look for a small coin in such a house, she would need to light a lamp even in the middle of the day.

The flooring of the typical Palestinian house would have also made the woman search diligently. Most houses had plain dirt floors where a small coin could easily lie hidden in the dust. The better houses had stone floors, but even there a coin might lie unnoticed between two stones. And so the woman looking for her lost coin would have had to give her house a thorough sweeping and a careful search.

That is why Jesus compared God with a woman: As the woman searched diligently for her lost coin, so God searches very diligently for lost people, for people who need God. That is why Jesus was glad to eat with tax collectors and with others outside of the religious establishment. He cared about people who were overlooked because they did not keep the Jewish religious law or because they were unconventional. He cared about people that others ignored.

In our own society today, people are still scorned or ignored for being outside of the social mainstream. People are still overlooked and all too easily lost even in our own churches. Those with physical, mental, or emotional difficulties are not always made welcome. Those of different ethnic backgrounds are not always included as equals. Even long-time members may sometimes feel left out and lost in their own churches.

When we feel lost and far from God, when we feel neglected and overlooked, it is easy to feel sorry for ourselves and to become discouraged. But Jesus' parable of the woman and the lost coin invites us to see the bigger picture. As the woman made a careful search for her coin that was easily lost, so God makes a careful search for us whenever we are lost. God longs to find us again, to welcome us back, and to rejoice over us.

Meditation Focus: In what ways do you feel lost within the church? In what ways do you think other people might feel lost?

Prayer: O God of the lost and lonely, we thank you that you search for us when we feel far from you. May we in turn search for others who are easily lost in our society and even in our churches. Help us to welcome them and rejoice over them, as you welcome and rejoice over all people who come to you. Amen.

Persistent Action, Persistent Prayer

Scripture Reading: Luke 18:1-8

Widows, orphans, strangers. These three groups of people received special attention in the law of the Old Testament. Since they had no family, God commanded the Israelite community to provide for them (Deut. 14:29; 24:19-21; 26:12-13). Since they were especially vulnerable to oppression, God commanded the Israelite community to see that they received justice (Deut. 27:19; Isa. 1:17; Jer. 22:3; Zech. 7:10).

But as the prophets would later point out, the people of Israel did not always practice what they heard preached to them (Jer. 7:5-7; Mal. 3:5). Too often widows, orphans, and strangers remained poor, defenseless, alone, and at the mercy of dishonest and greedy people.

In this parable recorded in the gospel of Luke, Jesus describes a widow of Israel who had apparently experienced some kind of injustice. She had no husband or other relative to defend her. She was likely poor, without money to hire a lawyer to present her case or to bribe the judge to act in her favor.

But in spite of her situation, this widow was neither weak nor helpless nor discouraged nor in despair. She was bold enough to present her own case before the judge, not just once, but numerous times. Convinced of the rightness of her case, she was courageous enough to keep on going even though the judge refused her time and time again. She was a woman of action.

I wonder if she was also a woman of prayer. Did she go to God with her case as often as she went to the judge? Did she draw on God's strength as she appeared before the judge again and again and again? How else could she have persisted as one lonely voice of protest before the formal authority of the court?

For many of us, prayer and action seem to be at opposite ends of the spectrum. We tend to think of prayer as sitting quietly, as we give thanks and make our requests known to God. We tend to think of action as physical movement, as we work, play, and interact with the world and with other people. We think of prayer and action as very distant relatives instead of twins belonging to the same family.

But in these verses, the gospel writer links the widow's persistent action with Jesus' words on persistent prayer. Here, as elsewhere in Jesus' life and ministry, the two go together. Jesus spent the night in prayer before he chose his twelve disciples (6:12). He spent the night in prayer before his arrest (22:41-42). He taught his disciples both to pray and to act (6:27-31; 10:2ff.).

Today in our own life and ministry, we also need both prayer and action. In fact, any situation that requires persistent action requires persistent prayer. Do we need persistent patience with a toddler or a teenaged son or daughter? Do we need persistent good humor to get ourselves through another day at the office? Do we need persistence in serving on a church committee or working in our community on housing, education, or other issues? Then we also need persistent prayer.

Our prayers help us to hear God as the guide and energizer of our action. Our actions give hands and feet to our prayers and give us ever more reason to pray. Action and prayer are inseparable. Each enriches and completes the other.

Like many widows in biblical times, we may have few material resources in the face of great needs. We may feel helpless or defenseless in the face of injustice. We may feel inadequate to do the tasks that God has given us. But like the widow in this parable, we need not be helpless or discouraged or in despair.

Instead, we can rely on God, the one who protects us more fearlessly than a husband, who defends us more courageously than sons and daughters. We can keep working like the widow, keep praying as Jesus urges us. And as we act and pray in faith, we can be sure that God strengthens and hears us.

Meditation Focus: Where do you need persistent action and persistent prayer in your own life? Do you tend to emphasize one at the expense of the other?

Prayer: God grant us the faith to be people of action and people of prayer, that we may practice justice and live faithfully on earth until Christ comes. Amen.

Reason to Weep

Scripture Reading: Luke 23:26-31

Even on his final journey—his journey to the cross—Jesus was again surrounded by people. Roman soldiers marched before him and beside him. Behind him, Simon of Cyrene carried the cross that Jesus was too weak to carry himself. Behind Simon came a group of unnamed women, loudly weeping and wailing at Jesus' coming death. And surrounding this terrible procession, a crowd of Passover visitors and curious bystanders filled the streets of Jerusalem.

The gospel writer tells us nothing of the identity of the unnamed women who followed after and mourned for Jesus. But since Jesus addressed them as "daughters of Jerusalem," they were probably not the same women who had followed Jesus from Galilee, but rather residents of Jerusalem. Some have suggested that these women were simply devout Jews performing a religious duty of mourning, but they may also have been women who had heard Jesus' teaching or experienced his healing and who now sincerely mourned his coming death.

At any rate, Jesus himself seemed to accept their weeping and wailing at face value, for he responded to them gently: "Daughters of Jerusalem, do not weep." His words were the very same words that he used to comfort the woman of Nain on the death of her only son. But this time Jesus went on to finish his sentence with a solemn warning: "weep for yourselves and for your children" (v. 28).

In his response to the daughters of Jerusalem, Jesus pronounced a great reversal. The women should not weep for him, but for themselves. Blessing would not rest on those with children, but on those who had none. The people would long for the mountains and the hills to cast down their great heights. The world would be turned upside down as destruction descended on Jerusalem.

Jesus ended his warning to these unnamed women with a proverb that has puzzled many scholars. While its precise meaning continues to be debated, the saying seems to imply an escalation of suffering and death. Green wood catches fire slowly; dry wood burns easily and is quickly reduced to ashes.

If this is the terrible present for Jesus, then what will the future hold in store for Jerusalem?

With this warning, Jesus seemed to relate his own death to the coming destruction of the city. Both were the result of sin and destruction in the world. Both were cause for weeping. Both meant great sorrow for the women of Jerusalem and for their children.

And so as Jesus journeyed toward the cross, he did not think only of his own suffering. He sought to comfort and to warn the women of Jerusalem who mourned his coming death. He thought of how they and their children and many others would suffer in the coming destruction of the city. Even in the face of his own death, Jesus had compassion on others.

Today we know that Jesus was crucified and rose again from the dead. Yet in our own way, we still remember and weep over Jesus' death. We may not sob and beat our breasts, but we commemorate his death in the bread and wine of communion, in the solemnity of Good Friday services, in night-long Easter vigils.

But as Jesus himself indicated, his death is not the only reason to weep. As Jesus did not isolate his death from the suffering of his world, so we should not isolate it from the suffering of our world. We need not weep only for Jesus, but also for the countless other men and women still condemned unjustly, for all those who suffer from sin and destruction. The same evil that sent Jesus to die also destroyed Jerusalem and continues to destroy our cities and people as well.

Like the unnamed women of Jerusalem who wept over Jesus and his cross, we too may weep over Jesus' death. But, like them, we are also challenged to think more widely of others who suffer. Jesus himself invites us to remember and weep.

Meditation Focus: What situations of sin and destruction in the world should you weep over? How do they relate to Jesus' death?

Prayer: O compassionate God, today as we remember the death of Jesus, we also remember the many people around the world who continue to suffer from sin and destruction. We weep for those women, children, and men, knowing that you weep too. We also ask for your help in turning our tears into concrete action, so that freedom and life may be at work in your world. Amen.

They Remembered

Scripture Reading: Luke 24:1-11

Once again Luke mentions several women by name: Mary Magdalene, Joanna, and Mary the mother of James. And once again he indicates the presence of a larger circle of unnamed women with an additional phrase: "and the other women with them" (v. 10). What can we know about these other women?

The story implies that both the named and the unnamed women were disciples of Jesus, for the two messengers from God tell them to remember Jesus' teaching about his death and resurrection. In Luke, Jesus gives this teaching only to his disciples (9:21-22, 44; 18:31-34). So if the women "remembered" Jesus' words (v. 8), they were most likely his disciples as well.

The context of this story provides further clues to the identity of these unnamed women. In the previous chapter, the same women are identified as those who had come with Jesus from Galilee and who had witnessed Jesus' burial (23:55). After our story and in the same chapter, they are identified by one of the disciples as "women of our group" (24:22).

As long-time disciples of Jesus, and as fellow travellers with the rest of the group, the women should have received a more serious hearing from the other disciples. But those who would soon become the apostles of the early church dismissed the women's testimony as foolishness. The women believed, but the men did not.

What made the two groups of disciples respond in such opposite ways? Was it only that the women saw the angels? Was it that the women were somehow more faithful to Jesus? No, the real difference was that the women remembered Jesus' words.

Like the other disciples, the women had not understood Jesus' talk about his death and resurrection. When they saw that Jesus' body was missing from the tomb, they still did not understand. And when they saw the two angels, they were filled not with faith, but with fear. It was only when they remembered Jesus' words that they were able to believe and leave the tomb with the news of Jesus' resurrection.

The same Greek word for "remember" is used six times in the gospel of Luke, and each time the word is linked with action. In Mary's song celebrating Jesus' birth, God remembers past mercy and helps Israel (1:54). In Zecharaiah's song, God remembers the past covenant and shows mercy on the people (1:72). In one of Jesus' parables, Abraham tells a rich man to remember his past luxury and so endure his agony (16:25). On the cross, a man asks Jesus to remember him, and Jesus affirms the man's presence in Paradise (23:42-43). In this story, the word is used twice with reference to the women (vv. 6, 8), who remember Jesus' words and then act on them.

So in the gospel of Luke, remembering is much more than a mental exercise. When the women remembered Jesus' words, they were not simply reminiscing or replaying his words over in their own minds. Their remembering was much more active. It was a remembering that moved them from fear to faith, from uncertainty to proclamation.

For us today, remembering also means action. To remember our manners means to act with consideration for others. To remember those who are sick means to visit them, to send a card, to pray. To remember those who are hungry means to eat responsibly and reduce waste, to support local food banks and national and international food programs. Remembering is not simply a sympathetic thought. Remembering means doing. In the same way, to remember God's love and forgiveness means to love and forgive ourselves and others. To remember Jesus' death and resurrection means to live a new life in the presence and power of God. Remembering changes the way we live.

And so as the unnamed women at the tomb remembered Jesus and his teaching, may we also remember Jesus and the power of his death and resurrection. As the women's remembering moved them to faith and proclamation, may our remembering also move us to fresh commitment and a new willingness to share the good news with others.

Meditation Focus: What things cause you to forget Jesus' teaching? What things cause you to remember? How does remembering affect the way you live?

Prayer: O God, we thank you for the example of these unnamed women who remembered Jesus' words and allowed his teaching to direct their lives. Grant us grace that we also may remember his words and live accordingly. In the name of Jesus, who died and rose again. Amen.

Living Water

Scripture Reading: John 4:1-42

Of all the unnamed women in the Bible, the Samaritan woman at the well is perhaps one of the most familiar. Although she appears only in the gospel of John, she has an entire chapter devoted to her story. Her encounter with Jesus is significant for its modelling of male-female and Jewish-Samaritan relationships, for its identification of Jesus as the living water and Messiah, and for its portrayal of the Samaritan woman as an evangelist to her own people.

The identity of the woman of Samaria as an evangelist seems to bind together all the other themes of the story. When Jesus reached across the invisible boundary dividing men and women and Jews and Samaritans, he set the woman free to reach across the invisible boundary dividing herself from the people of her town. When the woman understood Jesus to be the Messiah, she discovered living water not just for herself, but for her whole community. The story of this unnamed woman is the story of an evangelist.

As an evangelist, the Samaritan woman did not wait to be commissioned or ordained for public ministry. She did not wait for a committee on outreach to study the needs of her neighborhood. She did not even wait until she had finished her daily work of drawing water. Untrained, with her personal life still unresolved, this woman began to tell everyone about the good news that she had received from Jesus.

As a witness to her own people, the Samaritan woman proved to be more effective than Jesus' other disciples. When the disciples returned from the town, they brought back only bread. When the woman returned, she brought back people to listen to Jesus. The unnamed woman reached her Samaritan neighbors that the Jewish disciples would not or could not reach.

Like any good evangelist, the woman brought together people who needed Jesus with the living Messiah himself. She did not simply move the people to believe in Jesus on the strength of her own personal testimony and faith. Instead, she introduced them to the Living One, that they might hear Jesus' word for themselves and so develop a living and personal faith.

The woman's role as an evangelist is further highlighted by a number of specific phrases in the text. As Jesus called his disciples, so the woman called her neighbors to "come and see" (1:39; 4:29). As Jesus would later pray for his disciples and those who would believe "through their word," so the woman's neighbors believed "because of the woman's testimony" or, more literally, "through the woman's word" (17:20; 4:39). Jesus' own words to his disciples also seemed to imply that the woman was one of the "others" who labored, while the disciples were those who had entered her labor (4:38).

Today the fields are still ripe, and the reapers are still laboring to bring in the harvest. Some of God's workers might be thought of as official witnesses: pastors, teachers, missionaries, and evangelists. Others may be more unofficial witnesses as neighbors, parents, friends, and co-workers. But together, all are needed to spread the good news of Jesus Christ.

As followers of Jesus, we too have the privilege of being a part of this company of workers. Like the unnamed woman at the well, we may not be highly trained. We may not be part of any official missionary society or outreach committee. Our personal lives may not be perfect. But like this Samaritan woman, if we have met Jesus, we too may invite others to come and see.

As we go about this task of evangelism, the story of the woman at the well may be an encouragement to us. Like this unnamed woman, we too have a unique part to play in the mission of Jesus. We need not drink from our own wells any longer. Instead, we drink the living water from God, which is for us, for our community, and for the whole world. And then, refreshed, we may go out into our own fields as witnesses for Jesus Christ.

Meditation Focus: Who are the people that our own church leadership is unable or unwilling to reach with the good news? How might you help to reach those people?

Prayer: O God, we thank you for reaching beyond gender, ethnic, and other boundaries to invite all people to yourself. Help us to reach out to others in the same welcoming and life-affirming way. In the name of Jesus, the Living Water. Amen.

No More Double Standards

Scripture Reading: John 7:53-8:11

The scribes and the Pharisees knew better than anyone that the law of Moses commanded stoning for both the man and the woman caught in adultery. Yet when these leaders came before Jesus with their test case, they came with only the woman. By accident or by design, they had let her partner escape the public scrutiny and judgment they had planned for her.

In their eagerness to trap Jesus, the scribes and the Pharisees seemed unconcerned about this double standard. They gave no thought to its injustice or to its effect on the woman. They did not even seem to care that it went against the law of Moses which they claimed to follow. All that mattered to them was Jesus' reply. What would he do? What could he say?

At first Jesus gave no reply to the scribes and the Pharisees. He merely stooped down to write on the ground. Perhaps he wrote out his reply before he spoke, much as a judge might write out a verdict before announcing it aloud. Or perhaps, as some scholars suggest, Jesus wrote down all the sins of the scribes and the Pharisees who crowded around him.

Whatever Jesus wrote, it is clear from what he said that he rejected his opponents' double standard. But instead of focusing on the missing man in the case, Jesus spoke directly to the scribes and the Pharisees.

If they wanted strict justice, then so be it: only let the first stone come from the hand of one without sin. With these words, Jesus clearly held them to the same standard that they required of the woman. And to their credit, the scribes and the Pharisees accepted this saying. In silence, they walked away and left the woman alone with Jesus.

Once the men had gone, Jesus turned his full attention to the woman. He spoke to her directly and gave her the opportunity to comment on the scribes and the Pharisees' accusations. He accepted her statement that no one had condemned her, and then he let her go with the charge not to sin again. The sinless

Jesus—the only one able to carry out the letter of the law—refused to cast a single stone.

Unlike the scribes and the Pharisees, Jesus did not treat the woman as an object to be seized and held up to public scrutiny; Jesus treated her as a responsible person. He did not ask for a confession or lecture her or try to make her feel guilty. Instead, he spoke to her in the same direct manner and with the same respect that he had used with her accusers. For Jesus, there were no double standards.

Like the woman caught by the scribes and the Pharisees, we too have sometimes experienced the injustice of double standards. Like her, we have been judged by others who have ignored their own sinfulness. We have been held accountable to a stricter code of sexual conduct than the men in our lives. We have been paid less than men for the same work. We have had to prove ourselves more competent than men to do the same job.

But at times, we have also used double standards against other people and in our own favor. Sometimes we have judged others without recognizing our own sinfulness, condemning them and excusing ourselves for the very same things. Others may be "irresponsible," but we are simply "easy going." They may be "bad tempered," but we are understandably "over tired."

When we are on the receiving end, such double standards can be extremely painful; when we are on the giving end, they are generally deceptively—and conveniently—pain-free. But painful or pain-free, such double standards fall short of the integrity and honesty that characterized Jesus' relationships with others and that characterizes God's relationship with us. As Jesus treated both his Jewish opponents and this unnamed woman as responsible persons before God, so God treats us with that same single standard. God loves and respects each one of us and holds us accountable for the way we live.

Meditation Focus: What double standards have others imposed on you? What double standards have you imposed on others or used to your own advantage? What single standard should stand in their place?

Prayer: *O Holy God, we are overwhelmed by the respect and responsibility you grant us as people made in your image. We want to respond by living in ways that please you, and so we pray for the will and the strength to keep from sinning. Amen.*

The Challenge of Change

Scripture Reading: John 9:18-23

In the gospel record, Jesus intervenes at least twice in the lives of an unnamed mother and son: first, when he raises the son of the widow of Nain (7:11-17), and second, when he heals this man born blind. In both cases, Jesus takes the initiative to exercise his life-giving power. In both, he enters and transforms a situation of need.

But the reactions to these two miracles are very different. In the first story, the widow and those with her respond to Jesus' miracle with joy and praise. In this second story, however, the unnamed mother and those around her react in just the opposite manner. The Jewish leaders are angry that Jesus had performed the miracle on a sabbath day. And the man's mother, who really only enters the story at the summons of the Jewish authorities, seems almost paralyzed with fear.

Like the widow of Nain, perhaps this mother was also initially overcome with joy at her son's encounter with Jesus. How could she not have rejoiced that her son born blind could finally see the world around him? How could she stop herself from praising God and from telling everyone about the miracle? But by the time she and her husband face the Jewish leaders, she seems most reluctant to talk about what had happened.

Since the man's mother and father were not present when Jesus restored his sight, perhaps it is only understandable that they have little to tell the Jewish authorities. But they seem too quick to refer the religious leaders to their son, too quick to have the Pharisees ask him their questions instead. The gospel writer tells us why: the man's parents were afraid that they would be put out of the synagogue if they acknowledged Jesus' work in their son's life.

Such a consequence could not be taken lightly. After all, the synagogue stood at the heart of Jewish religious and social life. It was primarily a place for worship, but it also functioned as a school for children, as a gathering place for funerals, and even as a place for political assemblies. It was the center for almsgiving and distribution, a shelter where travellers and the poor could be fed and sometimes even housed. For the man's parents, being cut off from the synagogue would mean losing their place of worship, sacrificing the education of their other children, and being excluded from the rest of their community. No wonder they were afraid.

Suddenly their whole world and all their relationships had shifted. Their place in the synagogue was not as safe and secure as they had once thought. The Jewish leaders regarded them with suspicion. Even their son no longer needed them in the same way as before. For them, change meant not only new sight for their son, but new fears and new questions for themselves.

At times, we too may experience sudden change. Perhaps we receive healing of body or spirit. Perhaps we start school or receive a job promotion or marry or have a baby or move to a new town. Or perhaps someone else in our lives experiences a sudden change. At such times, we may rejoice and celebrate. We may even welcome the changes in our lives and in the lives of those around us as the work of God.

And yet we may also be very aware of the new fears and new questions that even the most positive changes bring to our lives. Will we be accepted in our new roles? Will we be equal to our new responsibilities? How will our relationships with others change? What parts of our old, safe world will we need to leave behind?

Like the parents of the man born blind, sometimes we let such fears crowd out our joy. Sometimes we want to retreat from the challenge of change. But like the widow of Nain, may we instead respond with joy and embrace the changes that come into our lives.

Meditation Focus: How has God been at work in your life or in the lives of loved ones? What changes has that meant for you?

Prayer: *O Sovereign God, we acknowledge your work in our lives and in the lives of others. Help us to welcome that work and to accept the change and growth that it means for us. Where we are too comfortable with our old way of life and too reluctant to change, rouse us to new commitment and enthusiasm. Where we are afraid, strengthen us to face the challenges you set before us. In the name of Jesus, who changes lives. Amen.*

Unity and Equality

Scripture Reading: Acts 6:1-7

Although the first Christians in Jerusalem were all Jews, they did not all share the same cultural and economic background. Some of them spoke primarily Aramaic. Others spoke Greek. Some were wealthy and had houses and lands to spare. Others were poor and dependent on the church's daily distribution of food. But in spite of these differences, the believers lived together as one body, bound by one Spirit and one faith. So great was their unity that the book of Acts says, "Now the whole group of those who believed were of one heart and soul, and no one claimed private ownership of any possessions, but everything they owned was held in common" (4:32).

As time passed, however, the cultural and economic differences within the community of faith increasingly challenged its unity and equality. In fact, these differences led to one of the very first disputes among the believers: the Greek-speaking, or Hellenist, members of the community complained that their poor widows were being overlooked in the daily distribution.

The Hellenists brought this situation to the attention of the apostles. The neglected and unnamed widows did not simply grumble among themselves and allow resentment to take root and grow. Their fellow Hellenists did not simply ignore the problem, nor did they go to the other extreme of attacking the apostles for their poor management. Instead, the Hellenist Christians willingly discussed the matter with their leaders.

For their part, the Hebrew apostles also responded in a prompt and positive manner. They took the complaint seriously and called the whole community together to settle it. At a general meeting they discussed the problem openly and suggested that the community appoint additional workers to ensure a fair distribution. Their solution satisfied both the Hebrews and the Greeks, both those who had provided the daily distribution and those unnamed widows who had been overlooked.

Today the church continues to face similar challenges to its unity and equality. There are still people who are overlooked within the church, people who fail to receive their fair share within the community of faith. Women, racial minorities, singles, and others continue to be under-represented in the leadership of the church. Those with special physical needs are not always considered in the planning of church buildings and activities. The poorer members of the church worldwide are still often neglected by the more wealthy members.

As those who are sometimes overlooked, we may hesitate to make our feelings known. We may fear being dismissed as complainers and troublemakers. We may fear appearing selfish or pushy. And so instead of openly expressing our concerns, we may whisper them to other dissatisfied members or maintain an increasingly angry silence. As leaders who work within the church, sometimes we have difficulty admitting that we have overlooked others. Instead of responding openly and honestly to criticism, we may become defensive.

But the experience of the Jerusalem Christians suggests a healthier response to disputes within the church. As members of the Christian community, we may work openly, constructively, and without resentment toward unity and equality in Jesus Christ. When we are overlooked, we may honestly share our feelings. When we feel discriminated against, we may honestly voice our concerns. As leaders, we too may respond to disputes in a positive manner. We may respect the opinions and feelings of others as our equals in Jesus Christ. We may address problems as they arise and be open to change.

As members and leaders of the church, let us respond honestly and openly to the challenges that face us. Let us seek to transcend the cultural, economic, and other differences that divide us. Let us work together for unity and equality in Jesus Christ, that God may be glorified and the church increase.

Meditation Focus: Have you ever felt overlooked within the church? Have you ever been criticized for overlooking someone else? How did you respond?

Prayer: O God, we pray for unity and equality within your community of faith. When disputes arise, may we discuss them openly and without resentment. May we listen to one another with respect and respond with genuine concern. So may we arrive at a solution that pleases you and seems good to all of us as members and leaders in the church. Amen.

God's Economy

Scripture Reading: Acts 16:16-24

Once Paul and Silas and their companions had reached Philippi, they wasted no time locating other God-fearers in the city. In their fellowship, Paul and his co-workers were made welcome and quickly accepted as ministers of God's word. But each time they went to their meeting place, a young girl would come after them and call out: "These men are slaves of the Most High God" (v. 17).

Now the young girl was a slave herself. She was a slave to her owners, for whom she worked as a fortune-teller. And she was also a slave to the fortune-telling spirit that possessed her. She had little choice but to do as her masters ordered, and even less choice but to obey the spirit within her. So day after day, she followed Paul and his companions and made her loud cry.

At first Paul managed to ignore the girl's disturbance. But as days went by without relief, he became increasingly irritated. One day as the girl again shouted after him, Paul turned and ordered the spirit to leave. In an instant, the girl was freed from her spirit of divination.

Unfortunately the girl was not freed from her masters. In spite of her new inner freedom, she remained very much a slave to her owners, and the institution of slavery remained very much a part of the economic system of the ancient world. It would not be until many years later that even Christian people would recognize the injustice of slavery.

Yet although the girl remained a slave, the narrator makes it clear that her economic relationship with her owners had already begun to change. Once the spirit had left her, the girl could no longer tell fortunes and would no longer earn the money her masters expected from her. With their hope of revenue gone, her owners became so angry that they seized Paul and Silas and had them imprisoned.

In the midst of these events, the young girl who started them was forgotten. Did she become a Christian? Did she join the church? Did her owners find a new way of using her to make money, or did they sell her? We do not know. We only know that as God's healing power had begun to change her life, it had also begun to change her economic relationships.

Like the unnamed slave girl in this story, we too may feel caught in an unjust economic system. We may not feel able to change the system or to choose as freely as we might wish. But God's transforming power in our lives means that our economic relationships can no longer be the same as they once were.

As God enters our lives, we too may find ourselves unable to perform certain jobs any longer. One person may feel led to resign from a military post or from a weapons manufacturing job. Another may feel unable to sell certain products or to follow certain business practices.

On the positive side, our new freedom in Christ may also affect our choice of vocation and the way we spend our money. We may take a position with less pay and longer hours, but greater service opportunity. We may practice a tithe or a graduated scale of giving that increases as our income increases. Even as we continue to wait for full economic freedom and justice, we can begin these new ways of being and doing.

Such changes in our economic affairs are bound to cause conflict. They may cause conflict with our employers and colleagues who have learned to depend on us in certain roles. They may cause conflict with our families and friends who may not understand our new convictions. They may cause inner conflict as we struggle with our new identities and new decisions.

As we do not know what happened to this unnamed slave girl, so we do not yet know what will happen to us. What new economic responsibilities and challenges will we take on? What new changes will we need to make? How will we deal with the conflicts we face? That part of our own story is still being written. Let us write it in the faith and freedom of Jesus Christ.

Meditation Focus: In what ways has your faith influenced your economic relationships?

Prayer: O Most High God, we acknowledge you as the God of both our inner and our outer lives, of our spiritual relationship with you and our economic relationships with others. Guide us in working at our vocations and using our money in ways that please you. In the name of Jesus, the way of salvation. Amen.

The Ministry of the Word

Scripture Reading: Acts 21:7-16

Here again we meet Philip, one of the seven men appointed to serve tables in Acts 6:5. Now, however, he no longer lives in Jerusalem and no longer waits on tables. Instead, he makes his home in Caesarea and serves the church as an evangelist.

At this time, Philip has four daughters who are described as virgins and as having "the gift of prophecy" (v. 9). But although the four women are described as prophets, they do not make any specific prophecy here. The prophetic word concerning Paul's future arrest is uttered instead by Agabus, a prophet from Judea. If the women played any part in confirming or supporting this prophecy, we are not told.

In the light of this silence, it is surprising that the four women are mentioned in this passage at all. Why does the narrator mention them when they play no real role in the story? Why mention their gift of prophecy when the only prophecy here is made by someone else?

It may be that Philip's four prophesying daughters are included here to continue the theme of prophecy from the gospel of Luke. In the gospel, both Mary the mother of Jesus and Zecharaiah the father of John the Baptist utter prophecies concerning their respective sons. When Mary and Joseph present Jesus at the temple, Simeon and Anna make prophecies over the young child. Now Acts introduces several more prophets: Philip's four daughters and Agabus.

A second reason for the women's appearance here may have been to acknowledge their role in the compilation of the book of Acts. Extra-biblical evidence from the early church historian Eusebius suggests that Philip's daughters may have been responsible for preserving and transmitting some of the stories of the early church. And so the writer of Acts may well have been indebted to the women for much of the information in the book.

Finally, the women may have been mentioned here simply because they were leaders in the early church. As prophets, they were part of the church's very foundation, second only to the apostles (1 Cor. 12:28; Eph. 2:20; 3:5; 4:11). Like their father Philip, they may have had little part in Paul's story beyond their role as his hosts. But, like Philip, perhaps they deserved special mention as leaders in the church.

As prophets, then, the daughters of Philip took part in the leadership of the early church and may have been responsible for some of the material we read in the Bible. Theirs was an on-going ministry so basic to the life of the church that it is mentioned here in Acts and remembered even years later by church historians.

We might also note that these four unnamed church leaders were not only women, but that they were also single. Neither their gender nor their marital status excluded them from leadership in the early church. Not all prophets were men. Not all prophets were married. Their suitability for ministry and church leadership rested with God's gifting.

Today the gift of prophecy is still God's gift to the church. It is exercised in many different ways: in foretelling and in forthtelling, in teaching and in preaching, in lay ministry and in ordained office. The ministry of God's word is still basic to the life and ministry of the church, still given to both men and women, to those who are married and to those who are single.

Like Philip's four prophesying daughters, some of us are also called to bring God's word to the church. We minister as occasional guest speakers or as regular preachers and teachers of the word. We speak to women and children and also to the whole church as the body of Christ. We address marriage and family issues as well as the broader areas of life and faith. As the word of God proclaims: "your sons and your daughters shall prophesy" (2:17, cf. Joel 2:28).

Meditation Focus: In what ways do you follow the tradition of Philip's four daughters in bringing God's word to the church? How might you encourage other women in the ministry of the word?

Prayer: O God, thank you for the four prophesying daughters of Philip, who brought your word to the church and who helped to lead it in its early life and ministry. May your sons and your daughters continue to prophesy today, and may we accept their word from you. In the name of Jesus, the Head of the Church. Amen.

Suggestions for Journaling

Journaling is simply thinking or praying on paper. You might make a poem or a prayer, a simple list or a letter, a sketch or a scribble. Use the meditation focus provided with each reading as the basis for your journaling, or try one of the following suggestions.

1. What new thought or information did you discover from reading the Scripture or the reflection?

2. How will your attitude or behavior be different after reading this reflection?

3. What emotions can you imagine the woman feeling? When have you ever felt the same way?

4. What decision faced the woman? What would you have done in her situation? How is it like or unlike decisions that you face in your own life?

5. What advice would you give to this unnamed woman? What advice do you think she would give to you?

6. Think of a situation or decision you currently face. What would this unnamed woman do in your place?

7. In what ways is this unnamed woman a good role model for you? In what ways would you want to avoid her example?

8. Imagine this unnamed woman as your friend. Write her a letter in which you connect your own circumstances and feelings with hers.

9. Write a psalm of praise or lament based on the story of this unnamed woman.

10. Write a prayer to God in response to this woman's story.

11. How could you respond to this woman's story in a practical way? Decide on a concrete action, write it down, and then do it this week. Follow up your action plan with another journal entry reflecting on your experience.

Suggestions for Small Group Use

If you are using this book with a small group, you may wish to consider one of the following ideas. Some of them require no preparation by group members; others require participants to do some reading and thinking in advance of your meeting. Be sensitive to the needs and abilities of your group, and plan your meetings with them in mind.

1. Read the Scripture passage and the reflection at your group meeting. Then ask each person to share the one statement or idea from the reading that struck her the most.

2. Use one or more of the journaling questions as discussion questions with your small group.

3. Ask one person in advance to retell in her own words the story of the unnamed woman in the Scripture reading. Have the story retold before you begin your discussion.

4. Ask each person to read the Scripture passage in advance and to bring an object to your meeting that might represent the unnamed woman in the story.

5. Select one of the books of poetry from the resource list: *Beginning with Mary, Eve and After,* or *The God of Sarah, Rebekah and Rachel.* Then choose a poem about the unnamed woman of the story, and use it as a discussion starter.

6. As the group leader, read the Scripture passage and reflection and decide on an overall theme for your meeting. Then plan your group time together around that theme. For example, if the theme is responding to our past, you might invite each participant to bring a photograph and to share it with the group. Or if the theme is prayer, you might want to plan a longer prayer time for your meeting.

7. Choose a psalm that goes with the theme of the story, and use it as a guided prayer. Good psalms for this include Psalms 4, 13, 16, 23, 41, 56, 84, 98, 121, 131.

8. If the members of your group are willing to spend the time, combine journaling and small group discussion. Between meetings, ask each member to read the Scripture and reflection and to keep her own journal. Then during your group meeting leave some time for participants to share excerpts from their journals if they wish. Encourage an atmosphere of openness and acceptance, and make it clear that all journal sharing is voluntary and should be kept confidential.

For Further Reading

The following list of books is just a small sample of the works consulted for *Remember Lot's Wife*. Some are poetry, some prose; some offer traditional interpretations of women in the Bible, some break new ground; all make stimulating reading.

Carlisle, Thomas John. *Beginning with Mary: Women of the Gospels in Portrait*. Grand Rapids: Eerdmans, 1986.

_____. *Eve and After: Old Testament Women in Portrait*. Grand Rapids: Eerdmans, 1984.

Carmody, Denise Lardner. *Biblical Women: Contemporary Reflections on Scriptural Texts*. New York: Crossroad, 1988.

Deen, Edith. *All of the Women of the Bible*. New York and Evanston: Harper and Row, 1955.

Grassi, Joseph A. *The Hidden Heroes of the Gospels: Female Counterparts of Jesus*. Minnesota: The Liturgical Press, 1989.

Nunnally-Cox, Janice. *Foremothers: Women of the Bible*. New York: The Seabury Press, 1981.

Pobee, John S. and Barbel von Wartenberg-Potter, eds. *New Eyes for Reading: Biblical and Theological Reflections by Women from the Third World*. Geneva: World Council of Churches, 1986.

Selvidge, Marla J. *Daughters of Jerusalem*. Scottdale: Herald Press, 1987.

Shenk, Barbara Keener. *The God of Sarah, Rebekah and Rachel*. Scottdale: Herald Press, 1985.

Stagg, Evelyn and Frank. *Woman in the World of Jesus*. Philadelphia: The Westminster Press, 1978.

Trible, Phyllis. *Texts of Terror: Literary-Feminist Readings of Biblical Narratives*. Philadelphia: Fortress Press, 1984.

Weems, Renita J. *Just a Sister Away: A Womanist View of Women's Relationships in the Bible*. San Diego: LuraMedia, 1988.